ROGER WILLIAMS UNIVERSITY LIBRARY

3 1931 00333 4322

CURRICULUM MATERIALS CENTER

War-Torn Bosnia

D1366764

ROGER WILLIAMS UNIV. LIBRARY

Other books in the History Firsthand series:

ROGER WILLIAMS UNIV. LIBRARY

War-Torn Bosnia

Helen Cothran, *Book Editor*

Daniel Leone, *President*
Bonnie Szumski, *Publisher*
Scott Barbour, *Managing Editor*
David M. Haugen, *Series Editor*

CURRICULUM MATERIALS CENTER

Greenhaven Press, Inc., San Diego, California

CMC
DR
1313.3
.W37
2002

#4765 8856   11/29/04

Every effort has been made to trace the owners of copyrighted material. The articles in this volume may have been edited for content, length, and/or reading level. The titles have been changed to enhance the editorial purpose.

No part of this book may be reproduced or used in any form or by any means, electrical, mechanical, or otherwise, including, but not limited to, photocopy, recording, or any information storage and retrieval system, without prior permission from the publisher.

Library of Congress Cataloging-in-Publication Data

War-torn Bosnia : history firsthand / Helen Cothran, book editor.
    p. cm. — (History firsthand series)
   Includes bibliographical references and index.
   ISBN 0-7377-0888-3 (pbk. : alk. paper) —
   ISBN 0-7377-0889-1 (lib. bdg. : alk. paper)
   1. Yugoslav War, 1991–1995—Bosnia and Hercegovina.
  2. Bosnia and Hercegovina—History—1992– I. Cothran, Helen.
  II. History firsthand series (Unnumbered)

DR1313.3 .W37   2002
949.703—dc21   2001040608
                                        CIP

CMC DR1313.3 .W37 2002
War-torn Bosnia

Cover photo: Associated Press
UNHCR/22021/05.1992/A. Hollmann, 154
UNHCR/22029/05.1992/A. Hollmann, 84
UNHCR/22031/05.1992/A. Hollmann, 66
UNHCR/22034/05.1992/A. Hollmann, 126
UNHCR/22035/05.1992/A. Hollmann, 172
UNHCR/22036/05.1992/A. Hollmann, 38

Copyright © 2002 by Greenhaven Press, Inc.
10911 Technology Place, San Diego, CA 92127

Printed in the USA

Contents

Chapter 1: The Causes of War

Chapter 2: Atrocities

Chapter 4: The Media

Chapter 5: The World's Response

Foreword

In his preface to a book on the events leading to the Civil War, Stephen B. Oates, the historian and biographer of Abraham Lincoln, John Brown, and other noteworthy American historical figures, explained the difficulty of writing history in the traditional third-person voice of the biographer and historian. "The trouble, I realized, was the detached third-person voice," wrote Oates. "It seemed to wring all the life out of my characters and the antebellum era." Indeed, how can a historian, even one as prominent as Oates, compete with the eloquent voices of Daniel Webster, Abraham Lincoln, Harriet Beecher Stowe, Frederick Douglass, and Robert E. Lee?

Oates's comment notwithstanding, every student of history, professional and amateur alike, can name a score of excellent accounts written in the traditional third-person voice of the historian that bring to life an event or an era and the people who lived through it. In *Battle Cry of Freedom*, James M. McPherson vividly re-creates the American Civil War. Barbara Tuchman's *The Guns of August* captures in sharp detail the tensions in Europe that led to the outbreak of World War I. Taylor Branch's *Parting the Waters* provides a detailed and dramatic account of the American Civil Rights Movement. The study of history would be impossible without such guiding texts.

Nonetheless, Oates's comment makes a compelling point. Often the most convincing tellers of history are those who lived through the event, the eyewitnesses who recorded their firsthand experiences in autobiographies, speeches, memoirs, journals, and letters. The Greenhaven Press History Firsthand series presents history through the words of first-person narrators. Each text in this series captures a significant historical era or event—the American Civil War, the

Great Depression, the Holocaust, the Roaring Twenties, the 1960s, the Vietnam War. Readers will investigate these historical eras and events by examining primary-source documents, authored by chroniclers both famous and little known. The texts in the History Firsthand series comprise the celebrated and familiar words of the presidents, generals, and famous men and women of letters who recorded their impressions for posterity, as well as the statements of the ordinary people who struggled to understand the storm of events around them—the foot soldiers who fought the great battles and their loved ones back home, the men and women who waited on the breadlines, the college students who marched in protest.

The texts in this series are particularly suited to students beginning serious historical study. By examining these firsthand documents, novice historians can begin to form their own insights and conclusions about the historical era or event under investigation. To aid the student in that process, the texts in the History Firsthand series include introductions that provide an overview of the era or event, timelines, and bibliographies that point the serious student toward key historical works for further study.

The study of history commences with an examination of words—the testimony of witnesses who lived through an era or event and left for future generations the task of making sense of their accounts. The Greenhaven Press History Firsthand series invites the beginner historian to commence the process of historical investigation by focusing on the words of those individuals who made history by living through it and recording their experiences firsthand.

Introduction

The war in Bosnia can be difficult to understand because there were many parties involved in the conflict and because the causes of the war were multiple, complex, and deep-rooted. Even after the war, commentators continue to argue about what caused it. The catastrophic results of the war, however, are easier to chronicle.

The Slavic People Diverge

In the simplest possible terms, the war in Bosnia—or Bosnia-Herzegovina, as the nation is properly called—was caused by deep-seated ethnic conflict, nationalism, and demagoguery. These causes are interrelated and, to be understood, require a brief explanation of the Balkan history leading up to the war. Bosnians share a common Slavic ancestry with the other Balkan peoples—many of whom they would come to fight with in the Bosnian war—but over time, Bosnians and other Slavs began to form distinct identities and establish separate political sovereignties. One factor that helped bring about this differentiation between Slavic groups was the constant invasions from empires outside the Balkans, most notably the Ottoman and Austro-Hungarian empires. At various times during a five-hundred-year period from the 1300s to the 1800s, the Ottoman and Austro-Hungarian empires conquered and ruled parts of the Balkan peninsula, including Bosnia.

Differences between the Slavs became more pronounced as each group adapted to different aspects of the conquerors' cultures. For example, many Bosnians adopted the Islamic religion from the Ottoman Turks, while Croats adopted Roman Catholicism from the Austro-Hungarians. Serbs—who resisted both foreign influences—adopted Orthodox Christianity from the Greeks, their southern neighbors. Although the distinct Slavic groups would sometimes band together to fight against outsiders, just as often they warred with one another for power, influence, and territory.

Each of the groups maintained sovereign nation-like states whenever they weren't being ruled by foreigners. Those burgeoning states eventually developed into the Balkan republics of Croatia, Bosnia, Slovenia, Albania, Montenegro, Macedonia, and Serbia, with its two republics, Vojvodina and Kosovo.

The Birth of Yugoslavia

As the centuries passed, resistance to domination by foreign empires and mistrust between Slavic groups increased. In 1914, Serb hostilities against the ruling Austro-Hungarian Empire resulted in the assassination of the heir to the Austrian throne, Archduke Ferdinand. A month later, Austria-Hungary declared war on Serbia, starting World War I.

When the Austro-Hungarian Empire was finally defeated in 1918 at the end of the war, the new country of the Kingdom of the Serbs, Croats, and Slovenes was formed, unifying the Slavic people. However, the new country was plagued with economic problems as a result of the war and experienced continued tension between the peoples of its various republics. In particular, Serbs and Croats vied for control of the nation. According to international studies professor Sabrina Petra Ramet, "Yugoslavia was created by Serbian bayonets"[1] and was dominated by Serbs for most of its history.

In 1929, Serbian king Alexander took the throne and began to rule as a benign dictator in order to get his nation under control. He renamed the country the Kingdom of Yugoslavia and tried to unite his people by redrawing territorial boundaries within the new nation and reorganizing the government. Many Serbs and Croats resented his dictatorship because it centralized power in Yugoslavia, which threatened to take power away from the individual republics. When the king was assassinated in 1934 by Croatian terrorists, his cousin, Prince Paul, took over the reign of Yugoslavia, but Paul's policies were much the same as his predecessor's and generated the same hostility.

Internal power struggles and economic problems prevented the new nation from successfully protecting itself against the Axis powers when they came into power in 1939 at the onset of World War II. Yugoslav officials decided to align themselves with the strongest of the warring parties—Germany—as a way to protect the country, but many Yugoslavs—especially Serbs—rebelled. They did not want to be allies with the Germans, whom they excoriated for invading foreign lands and slaughtering Jews. Anti-German demonstrations in the Serbian city of Belgrade resulted in Adolf Hitler ordering the German air force to bomb the city on April 6, 1941. When the Germans, Italians, Hungarians, and Bulgarians attacked Yugoslavia in the wake of the bombing, the Yugoslav army collapsed, and the Axis powers took control of the country.

The invasion of Yugoslavia during World War II set off deadly internal conflicts between the different republics. When Germany—long sympathetic to the Croats, who claimed a shared ancestry—created the independent republic of Croatia, extreme Croatian nationalists, called the Ustase, began to brutally expunge all non-Croats from their new nation. Two Serbian resistance groups—the Chetniks and the Partisans—developed to combat the Ustase. The Chetniks were as ruthless as the Ustase and began slaughtering all non-Serbs in the Balkan region. The Partisans, led by communist Josip Broz—later called Marshal Tito—were a more moderate resistance organization, and they ultimately prevailed in the struggle for power. With the help of the Allies, the Partisans defeated the Germans and disbanded the Ustase and Chetnik forces. Tito and his communist allies took control of Yugoslavia in 1945.

Communist Yugoslavia

Although the conflicts that resulted in the massacre of hundreds of thousands of Yugoslavs during World War II—most of whom died at the hands of other Yugoslavs—still rankled,

Yugoslavs enjoyed relatively peaceful and prosperous times under Tito. Tito had been expelled from the communist alliance, Cominform, by Soviet leader Joseph Stalin in 1948 for not complying with standard communist principles. This separation freed the Yugoslav leader to adopt a more free-market version of communism. Under Tito's communist regime, people could own land, travel abroad, and receive uncensored Western publications. Access to health care and education improved, and cities began to prosper. Tito disapproved of religion because he thought it divided people, but he did not severely punish those who were determined to practice their faith, although those who were determined to do so were relatively few.

The country's political structure also helped establish peaceful relations between its republics. Yugoslavia under Tito was a federation containing six republics and two provinces. Each of the republics and provinces was governed by a president who, similar to a U.S. governor, had some power within his own republic but was required to obey and uphold laws as established by the federation. Federal law and a common language helped bind the diverse Slavic peoples together, and in spite of what had happened in the past, Yugoslavs got along fairly peacefully with one another. To build a strong national identity, Tito encouraged the people to be proud of being Yugoslavian. At the same time, however, he adamantly opposed any identification with a particular republic and quashed any public expressions of ethnic pride. Tito believed that such sentiments seriously threatened the cohesion of the federation.

Tensions Mount

When Tito died in 1980, the Communist Party weakened and new parties came to the fore. This dispersal of power quickly resulted in the erosion of the peace and prosperity that Tito had established during his reign. The federal government was now based on a revolving presidency; a different president from each of the republics and provinces took a turn at governing the country for one year. As a result of the revolving presidency, presidents began to wield more power than they had under Tito's communism.

With power devolving to the presidents—each with the well-being of his own republic in mind—Yugoslavia as a federation began a rapid descent into chaos. The rotating presidency turned out to be a weak vehicle for ruling a nation. Centralized power went to the most powerful of the republics, Serbia. As Serbian power grew, the other republics began to consider seceding from the Yugoslav union and forming their own independent nations. They argued that Serbian president Slobodan Milosevic "was a unifying force among Serbs but a divisive factor in Yugoslavia as a whole."[2]

The post-Tito government provided these discontented republics with ways to pursue independence. With the end of Tito's regime, Yugoslavia had established free elections and a multiparty system of government. Unfortunately, the Yugoslav states did not use these democratic tools to further democratize the country but, rather, used them to enhance their own power. For example, "free elections" in Serbia were now being rigged by Milosevic's party to ensure that the Serbian president stayed in power. Other republics did the same. In addition, the "free press" could now be used by those in favor of separation to tell lies about other republics and spread hate. Either fearing or simply not knowing what to believe about their neighboring republics, the people often fell back on age-old ethnic ties to determine who could or could not be trusted.

The presidents who gained the most power under the new democratic scheme were those who belonged to the ethnic groups that were in the greatest majority within the federation and those who were willing to use that fact to their advantage. For example, Milosevic was the most powerful Balkan leader in part because Serbs constituted a majority in Yugoslavia. Milosevic would become one of the main players in the Bosnian war, in addition to Croatia's President Franjo Tudjman and Bosnia's President Alija Izetbegovic. Milosevic and Tudjman used the new decentralized government to gain power, and they manipulated the growing ethnic-based nationalism of their people in order to win political support. With Tito out of the way and one-party rule extinguished, Milosevic and Tudjman could push for policies that would benefit their respective republics rather than work on behalf of the federation.

Tito's belief that ethnic pride and nationalism would tear the federation apart proved well founded. Many people began to celebrate their republic's history and their ethnic identities. Without the manipulation of ambitious leaders, however, such sentiments would likely not have resulted in war. Unfortunately, political leaders were quick to take the pulse of the populace and began to ardently encourage these sentiments. What's more, they began to manipulate the people of their respective republics into believing that they were superior to other Yugoslavs and that people in the other republics were a threat to them. Many demagogues even reminded them of the atrocities committed during World War II to gain support for their nationalistic plans. Milosevic and Tudjman went so far as to discuss dividing up the republic of Bosnia between them in order to reclaim portions of Bosnia that they believed had been stolen from them when Tito redrew territorial boundaries to establish the federation. Bosnian president Izetbegovic, presiding over the most ethnically mixed republic in the federation, for the most part remained silent on the issue of ethnic pride and nationalism. But as he began to feel more and more threatened by his neighbors' ambitions to carve up his republic, he considered withdrawing Bosnia from the federation and establishing an independent nation.

Secession and Independence

Izetbegovic was not the first to consider declaring independence from Yugoslavia. As the tensions between the republics continued to mount, both Slovenia and Croatia devised plans to withdraw from the federation. However, Milosevic was vociferously opposed to their leaving the union, for he could see that their departure would seriously weaken the federation, thereby undermining his own power in Europe. Consequently, the Serbian president decried all moves toward independence as illegal moves of secession, amounting to civil war. He argued that Slovenia and Croatia had a legal tie to Yugoslavia and could not simply break that tie when it suited them.

Despite Milosevic's protests, on June 25, 1991, Croatia and Slovenia each declared their formal independence from Yugoslavia. The Serb-dominated Yugoslav government reacted to these acts of secession by sending the Yugoslav National Army (JNA) to Slovenia in an attempt to force that republic back into the union. However, the Slovenian army was able to quickly repulse the JNA forces. There were few Serbs living in Slovenia, so the Yugoslav government saw little point in fighting Slovenian independence any longer. Conversely, Croatia was less well-armed, and a large minority of Serbs lived there. Letting Slovenia go, the JNA then turned its attention to Croatia, sending in troops in an effort to force the republic to return to the federation. Moreover, the JNA aided Serbs living in Croatia who had already taken up arms to protest Croatia's declaration of independence.

Croatian Serbs, who constituted a majority in Croatia's Krajina region, began an armed conflict in an attempt to wrest control of the area from Croatia. In part they were protesting the human rights violations that the nationalistic Croats had perpetrated against them as independence drew near. Serbs had been slaughtered and their homes torched. Even in other areas of Croatia, Serb employees were fired and Serb tenants evicted by Croatians who were sympathetic to Croatia's nationalist cause. Not surprisingly, Croatian Serbs feared that they would have no civil rights under the newly independent Croatia.

With the help of the JNA—which was becoming increasingly Serb-dominated as Slovenian and Croatian soldiers left it to join armies in their own countries—Croatian Serbs were able to gain control of the Krajina region and declare it the Croatian Serb Republic. In the meantime, the Serbs began to expunge non-Serbs from the region and hold it against the Croatian army. During the Croatian war, between

6,000 and 10,000 people died as a result of the fighting, 400,000 were left homeless, and material damage was estimated at $18 billion. Croatia's President Tudjman, an ardent nationalist, denounced the Croatian Serbs for trying to break apart his country.

The war was finally ended in 1992 by a cease-fire agreement brokered by the United Nations (UN), and UN peacekeeping forces were sent to the area to maintain the peace that both sides had agreed to. This UN intervention was the first time that other nations had become involved in the growing Balkan conflicts. The lack of outside intervention proved to be a topic of intense debate throughout the wars in Croatia and Bosnia. In particular, Bosnians criticized the United Nations and other countries for not helping them when war finally arrived on their soil.

Bosnia's Bid for Independence

In spite of Slovenia's and Croatia's difficult transitions toward independence, two other republics, Bosnia and Macedonia, also decided to secede from Yugoslavia. In a move that some critics have blamed for fueling the Balkan wars, the UN and many Western countries recognized Slovenia and Croatia as sovereign states, thus bolstering bids for self-determination in other Yugoslav republics. Macedonia—only about 2 percent of which was Serbs—was allowed to secede without any armed resistance. But when Bosnia—whose population was about one-third Serb—seceded in March 1992, the JNA immediately began to help Bosnian Serbs fight the secession. The beginning of the Bosnian war was in many ways a mirror of the Croatian war, but in Bosnia, the war would go on for three years.

The man who some analysts claim was the most responsible for the Bosnian war was Bosnian Serb Radovan Karadzic. Even before the war started, as Bosnian officials discussed their plans to leave Yugoslavia, Karadzic declared a large portion of Bosnia—which contained a Serb majority—as the Serb Republic of Bosnia, or Republika Srpska. An ardent Serb nationalist, Karadzic told Bosnian Serbs that they would be oppressed by the Muslim majority if Bosnia seceded from Yugoslavia. History professor Ivo Banac argues that the Bosnian Serb community was "essentially subverted and presented with a reinterpretation of its own history: namely that it had always been on the receiving end of Muslim domination in Bosnia-Herzegovina and that its future and security lay within a 'Greater Serbia.'"[3] With the help of a ruthless general named Ratko Mladic and the JNA, Karadzic succeeded in laying siege to the capital city of Sarajevo—which contained a Muslim majority—taking control of hundreds of villages within the borders of his newly declared republic, and slaughtering hundreds of thousands of Muslims.

Karadzic garnered support for his war by claiming that the Muslims in all the Balkan nations were going to populate and eventually take over the whole of Europe and make people convert to Islam. Karadzic was merely echoing a sentiment that had become popular in neighboring Serbia. Professor Ramet reports that a Serb from Belgrade claimed "Albanian Muslims and Bosnian Muslims are in this together. They have big families in order to swamp Serbia and Yugoslavia with Muslims and turn Yugoslavia into a Muslim republic. . . . They will continue to advance until they have taken Vienna, Berlin, Paris, London—all the great cities of Europe. Unless they are stopped."[4] Unfortunately, many Bosnian Serbs also shared these fears and believed whatever Karadzic said on the radio about the Muslim threat. Bosnian Serbs were already worried that they would lose all the advantages they had enjoyed while being part of Serb-dominated Yugoslavia. Statistics from 1991 show that Serbs made up only about 31 percent of the population in Bosnia, Croats were 17 percent, and Muslims were nearly 44 percent. With Bosnian independence, Serbs suddenly found themselves a minority in their new country.

When the fighting began in the spring of 1992, Karadzic encouraged his people to believe that they were being attacked by this Muslim majority. In reality, the Muslims were merely trying to defend themselves from General Mladic's brutal army. The Muslims were at a decided disadvantage throughout the war because they did not have a regular military. As Karadzic's forces began to take over parts of Bosnia, Muslim men from all walks of life—doctors, shopkeepers, barbers—formed an "irregular" army and fought on the Bosnian government's behalf. In addition, many Bosnian Serbs and Croats who were sympathetic to the Bosnian government fought alongside the Muslims. Unfortunately, such an amalgam of soldiers did not make for an especially effective fighting force, although reports from the period indicate that the "irregulars" fought with bravery and tenacity.

Another serious problem that the Muslims faced was their lack of access to arms and ammunitions. The reason for their plight was simple. In September 1991, the United Nations had imposed an arms embargo against Yugoslavia in part to forestall any armed conflicts in the region. Although Bosnia was technically no longer part of Yugoslavia once it seceded, the UN refused to lift the arms embargo against it. Most Western nations were reluctant to give arms to any party in the conflict, arguing that such an action would only lengthen the war. Many critics of this policy, however, contend that the arms embargo was the single most important factor in lengthening the war. They claim that if the Muslims had been sufficiently armed, they could have successfully fought the Serbs and ended the war quickly. However, as a result of the embargo, the best that the Muslims could do was keep from being obliterated. Conversely, the Bosnian Serbs could continue their campaign against their weaker enemy indefinitely. While the Bosnian government was forced to try to smuggle small arms in from Islamic countries such as Iran, the Bosnian Serbs not only shared the resources of the JNA, they also had help from their powerful ally, Serbia.

Hungry Nationalists

Throughout the wars in Croatia and Bosnia, Serbian president Milosevic denied any involvement in the conflicts. He repeatedly told Western journalists and diplomats that all he wanted was peace. Yet many analysts argue that Milosevic did in fact aid the Croatian and Bosnian Serbs because he wanted to add the areas they conquered to a Serbia-controlled Yugoslavia. Western diplomats maintained that, at the very least, Milosevic could have stopped the war in Bosnia. However, Milosevic claimed that "it's unfair to make Serbia responsible for the actions of a million and a half Bosnian Serbs. I have no influence over Karadzic."[5] The preponderance of evidence counters Milosevic's claims of neutrality, however. For example, numerous photographs from the period show the Serbian army delivering weapons to the Bosnian Serbs. Of course, as Ramet contends, Milosevic "did not create the hatreds in Yugoslavia. He catered to them, manipulated them, and amplified them."[6]

While the fighting commenced, political analysts also thought it odd that Croatian president Franjo Tudjman did not condemn Milosevic for his hand in the war in Croatia or denounce him for trying to stop Bosnia's bid for the same political autonomy that Croatia had pursued. To be sure, Tudjman denounced the Croatian Serbs for trying to take Croatia's Krajina region, and he ruthlessly tried to stop them. But the president never blamed Milosevic for helping them. On the contrary, Tudjman said he could trust Milosevic. Upon closer examination, however, Tudjman's stance was not surprising. In March 1991, he and Milosevic discussed dividing up Bosnia between them. In essence, the Croatian president did not want to jeopardize his alliance with the Serbian leader because he needed Milosevic's help to carve up Bosnia. Tudjman publicly conceded that he was willing to let Milosevic have the majority of Bosnia because he controlled it anyway, but Tudjman was going to take control of the areas heavily populated by Croats. During a 1993 press conference, Tudjman said, "The acceptance of Bosnia-Herzegovina as a unity state would endanger the survival of the Croatian people, as well as the strategic interests of the Republic of Croatia. Therefore, the Croatian people will hold onto those regions in Bosnia-Herzegovina in which Croats constitute a majority."[7] Both Tudjman and Milosevic justified their claims by contending that Bosnia had been artificially created by Tito, who had stolen land that belonged to Croatia and Serbia in order to establish Bosnia's borders.

Tudjman's nationalist ambitions made Bosnia's problems significantly worse. While fighting the Bosnian Serbs in the eastern part of the country, the Bosnian government had depended on Croatia—which was located to the north and west—to help them obtain food, arms, and ammunition. However, when Bosnian Croats declared their independence from Bosnia and established the Herceg-Bosna Republic in July 1992, Croatia cut its alliance with Bosnia and began to support the Bosnian Croats in fighting against Muslims and expunging them from the Herceg-Bosna Republic. Not only was Bosnia's access to outside supplies essentially cut off, but the newly independent nation was now fighting two wars, one against the Serbs and one against the Croats.

Ethnic Cleansing

Many non-Serbs in Bosnia were quickly annihilated in the initial stages of the war. Serbs—and to a lesser extent, Croats—began conducting "ethnic cleansing" to expunge Muslims from territories under their control. In most instances, the Bosnian Serb Army (BSA) would enter a village, shoot most of the Muslim men, and take the rest to concentration camps, where they were starved, tortured, and often killed. The Muslim women were often sent to rape camps, where they were repeatedly raped by BSA soldiers. Many analysts believe that the soldiers who committed the rapes were obeying orders from Karadzic, who wanted Muslim women impregnated by Serbs in order to enlarge the Serbian population in Bosnia. The remaining women and children of the village were loaded into cattle cars and shipped to refugee centers. Those who survived the journey in the airless, cramped cars often grew ill as a result of the unsanitary and crowded conditions of the camps. After all of a village's residents were removed, BSA soldiers then set fire to many Muslim buildings. If any Serbs lived in the village, their homes were spared, and the BSA encouraged them to claim any Muslim property that they coveted. When Western journalists who were covering the war first publicized this "ethnic cleansing" at the hands of Serbs and Croats, people in Europe and the United States began to urge their governments to do something to stop it. However, the war continued with no outside intervention and no end to the atrocities.

In large cities such as Sarajevo, BSA tactics were different because they met stronger resistance. The army besieged Sarajevo for over two years, bombing buildings, firing at civilians, and preventing supplies from reaching the city. Not a single building was left without damage, and many were completely destroyed by mortar shells and artillery. Sarajevo's library, its newspaper building, and the Olympic village where the 1984 Winter Olympic Games were held were all annihilated. Residents who walked in the streets were often killed by mortar shells or sniper fire. Electricity and water were cut off, and food became scarce. Without the aid of Western journalists—who delivered letters and brought food and medical supplies to the people—and UNPROFOR (the United Nations Special Protection Force), which was sent to Bosnia in the spring of 1992, many more Sarajevans would have died. In all, more than ten thousand lost their lives during the siege, and many more were permanently wounded.

Many commentators believe that Sarajevo was besieged in order to draw attention away from the genocide that was being conducted in rural regions of the country. However, Karadzic claimed that he wanted to divide Sarajevo into three ethnic cantons divided by a Balkan version of the Berlin Wall because, according to him, Serbs, Croats, and Muslims could never live together in one city. Ironically, all three were living together in the city at the time of the siege and often cooperated with one another in order to survive.

Little Help from the West

While UNPROFOR helped protect the humanitarian aid efforts designed to bring medicine and food to the people of

Sarajevo and other besieged cities, critics accused the UN of not doing anything to stop the war. Bosnians were especially critical. When Bosnia's president asked for UN protection following Bosnia's declaration of independence, he believed that the UN would protect Bosnia from reprisals from the Bosnian Serbs and Croats. However, Izetbegovic overestimated the role that the UN was willing to play in the conflict. The UN typically does not take sides in a conflict. A traditional UN peacekeeping operation is designed to enforce a peace already established. For example, UN peacekeeping forces were sent to Croatia only after the cease-fire agreement was signed, and their role was strictly to enforce that peace. When UNPROFOR established itself in Bosnia, it was operating on the same neutrality mandate. In fact, UNPROFOR was instructed to view Serbs, Croats, and Muslims as equally responsible for the war. UNPROFOR's role was strictly to protect the aid effort. Sarajevans began to deride UNPROFOR soldiers to their faces for merely "watching the carnage," and the residents came to view the UN's white armored vehicles and blue helmets as symbols of the world's refusal to come to their aid.

Indeed, for most of the war, no foreign country sent troops to fight in Bosnia. One reason for the West's inaction was that, with the disintegration of the Soviet Union in 1990, the communist threat to Europe appeared to be over. The West no longer viewed Yugoslavia—which it had long seen as a bulwark against the spread of Soviet-style communism—as an important concern. Individual nations had other reasons for noninvolvement. The United States, for example, was reluctant to enter a conflict that, like the Vietnam War, would be hard to win and from which it would be difficult to extricate itself. Yet many journalists and Western diplomats urged the West to intervene on behalf of the Bosnian government. Warren Zimmermann, the U.S. ambassador to Yugoslavia from 1989 to 1992, argues that "Bosnia was a clear case of aggression; [the United States] had a moral, perhaps even a legal, obligation to deal with it."[8] Many nations in the West sent diplomats to Bosnia to broker a peace agreement in an effort to avoid sending in troops to end the conflict. But diplomatic efforts such as the 1993 Vance-Owen and Geneva plans failed dismally and contributed to the devastation of Bosnia by prolonging the war. However, the UN did help broker a cease-fire agreement between the Bosnian Croats and the Bosnian government in February 1994.

The End of the War

Bosnia's war with Croatia ended with the 1994 cease-fire, but its war with the Bosnian Serbs continued until November 1995, when the UN was able to broker a peace agreement. NATO's bombing of strategic Bosnian Serb locations had helped bring the Bosnian Serbs to the negotiating table. All parties signed the Dayton Peace Accords in Dayton, Ohio, in November 1995, but by then, nearly 200,000 Bosnians were dead. The accords resulted in the division of Bosnia along ethnic lines. Bosnian Serbs were given much of the land that they had taken, which was officially recognized as Republika Srpska. Another autonomous region called the Muslim-Croat Federation was also formed, and NATO-led troops were stationed in the remaining territory of Bosnia to monitor compliance with the accords.

The UN international war crimes tribunal that was established continues to try war criminals such as Dragoljub Kunarac and Radomir Kovac, who were convicted in 2001 of sexually enslaving Bosnian Muslim women and girls. The tribunal has also accused Radovan Karadzic and Ratko Mladic of being war criminals for their involvement in ethnic cleansing, but neither man has yet been captured and tried. Milosevic was also indicted by the tribunal for war crimes committed in a later conflict with Serbia's province, Kosovo. Since Milosevic is no longer president of Serbia, his influence in the region has declined, and in March 2001, he was arrested on charges of corruption by Serbian Special Forces. Many analysts claim that his arrest will ultimately result in his being turned over to the tribunal to stand trial for his involvement in the Balkan conflicts.

Many of those responsible for atrocities committed during the Bosnian war have met with justice, and peace has been established for now. However, the war has left devastation in its wake. Of course, the greatest consequences of Bosnia's war are borne by the warring parties themselves. Both Bosnia and Croatia suffered devastating death tolls. The economies of all three republics involved in the conflict were severely damaged. The infrastructure in much of Bosnia has to be entirely rebuilt, and unemployment in the country has hit an all-time high. Perhaps the most serious consequences of the war, however, are the psychological scars it has left on the survivors. If peace between the various peoples in the Balkan region was sometimes difficult to achieve before the Bosnian war, that task has been made significantly harder at the war's conclusion.

Indeed, the war has left a multitude of thorny problems, many of which are borne by the individuals who were displaced by the conflict. Some refugees have returned to their native villages to try to rebuild their lives, but others cannot—their villages are now located in Republika Srpska or have been completely destroyed. Many who fled the country, such as Ranka and Zoran Vukmanic, are trying to make a life for themselves in other countries such as the United States. Although they find life in their new country strange and at times difficult, the Vukmanics do not want to return to Bosnia. They believe that the Muslim, Croat, and Serb governments were equally culpable for the destruction of their country and contend that Balkan leaders, in their quests for power, will continue to use the ethnic tensions that began more than five hundred years ago to pit the Bosnian people against one another.

The Bosnian war is much more than a history of maps, secession, and nationalist slogans. It is a history of individuals like Ranka and Zoran Vukmanic and their children. Bosnia's population is either dead, scattered throughout the world, or in Bosnia, trying to build hope from the ruins. Those who lost limbs from wartime amputations are constant reminders of the atrocities that occurred. Others whose loved ones died in the war struggle with their feelings of loss and their hatred for those responsible. Most survivors suffer post-traumatic stress disorder, an illness that includes severe depression and crippling stress. Others remain refugees, uprooted and homeless. The worst damage done during the Bosnian war cannot be repaired with bricks and mortar, for it is carried in the minds of the survivors.

Savage Killers or Victims?

Many commentators claim that the Bosnian war is evidence of the warlike nature of the Balkan peoples. They argue that the Balkans is an unusually savage place where people are uniquely unforgiving and contentious. However, others contend that the internal conflicts that have historically plagued the region are not much different from those that plagued other countries. They point out that England's history, for example, is a chronicle of ceaseless wars between ruling families. Warren Zimmermann argues that "Balkan genes aren't abnormally savage" and discounts the theory that Yugoslavia was uniquely violent. He writes, "Europe, taken as a whole, has endured two civil wars in [the twentieth] century, involving sixty million deaths, including the genocidal annihilation of six million European Jews."[9] And Ramet claims, "Muslims, Serbs, and Croats had lived in peace for most of the 500 years they cohabited in Bosnia."[10]

Indeed, some analysts maintain that the respect between the Yugoslav people can be illustrated by examining the interaction of the various ethnic groups within Bosnia. At the time of the Bosnian war, for example, one-third of all Bosnian families were headed by parents of different ethnicities. In Yugoslavia as a whole, over a fifth of its citizens were members of ethnically mixed families as of 1991. Many experts contend that such marriages produced mixed children who did not consider themselves as belonging to one ethnic group or the other, but merely Bosnian. Villages often contained a mixture of the three groups, and villagers often did not know—or care—what ethnicity their neighbors were. In addition, in the twentieth century, the people of Bosnia were not particularly religious, so religious differences were not especially divisive. In a poll taken in 1985, only 17 percent of Bosnians reported a religious affiliation.

Big cities like Sarajevo were made up of many different people, and such diversity was not only accepted but viewed as a model for a multicultural Bosnia. Many experts contend that what happened when Bosnia declared independence in 1992 had less to do with "ethnic tension" among individual Bosnians and more to do with what journalist Ed Vulliamy calls "the resurrection in our time of the dreams and aggrieved historical quests of two great Balkan powers of medieval origin, Serbia and Croatia."[11] Unfortunately, as a result of the war, Bosnians now mistrust other Balkan peoples more than before, which makes them vulnerable to the manipulations of future demagogues along the lines of Milosevic, Tudjman, and Karadzic.

Notes

1. Sabrina Petra Ramet, *Balkan Babel.* Boulder, CO: Westview Press, 1992, p. 40.

2. Ramet, *Balkan Babel,* p. 27.

3. Quoted in Rabia Ali and Lawrence Lifschultz, eds., "Separating History from Myth: An Interview with Ivo Banac," *Why Bosnia?* Stony Creek, CT: Pamphleteer's Press, 1993, p. 135.

4. Ramet, *Balkan Babel,* p. 185.

5. Quoted in Warren Zimmermann, *Origins of a Catastrophe.* New York: Random House, 1996, p. 198.

6. Ramet, *Balkan Babel,* p. 300.

7. Quoted in Ramet, *Balkan Babel,* p. 210.

8. Zimmermann, *Origins of a Catastrophe,* p. 216.

9. Zimmermann, *Origins of a Catastrophe,* p. 209.

10. Ramet, *Balkan Babel,* p. 243.

11. Ed Vulliamy. *Seasons in Hell.* New York: St. Martin's Press, 1994, p. 5.

Chapter 1

The Causes
of War

Item(s) . . . . 04/24/44.

TITLE: War. Turn Points
CALL #: CML UB155.5 . W37 2000
BARCODE: 31111011441
DUE DATE: 11 03 11
LOCATION: RWU CML
COPY : 1

Roger Williams University
Bristol, RI

Chapter Preface

Many of the conflicts between Serbs, Croats, and Muslims in Bosnia can be traced back to World War II. When Germany and Italy divided Yugoslavia among themselves in 1941, alliances within the nation shattered along ethnic lines.

Germany declared a new independent state of Croatia in 1941, and most Croatians celebrated the new state, believing that Croatia would finally be free of Serbia's dominance. Sympathetic to the Croats—who claimed to share a common ancestry with the Germans—Germany set up leader Ante Pavelic to govern the new state, and under his command the extremist nationalists called Ustase began to brutally expunge all Serbs from Croatia. Thousands of Serbs were massacred, and non-Croats, including Germans, began to complain about Ustase brutality.

As the death toll mounted, two Serbian resistance groups rose up against the Ustase and anyone else who supported the independent state of Croatia. One of these groups, the Chetniks, wanted to create a homogenous Serbia and tried to expunge Croats and Muslims from regions in Bosnia. The second group, simply referred to as Partisans, led by future Yugoslav leader Tito, wanted a united, communist Yugoslavia, and they began to fight against the Chetniks as well as the Ustase.

Muslims in Bosnia fell victim to both the Ustase and the Chetniks. The Muslims generally favored Croatia, and some Muslims even joined the Ustase in order to avenge the destruction of thousands of Muslims by the Chetniks from 1941 to 1942. The Muslims were also killed by the Ustase, however, and in November 1942, the Muslims addressed a memorandum to Adolf Hitler which demanded that the Ustase massacres stop and requested political autonomy in

Bosnia. In response, Germany created a Muslim division in its army. The Muslims believed that this force had been created to protect Muslims in Bosnia, but, instead, the division was commanded to commit murders and other crimes against the local Serb population.

On April 6, 1945, Bosnia came under the control of Tito's Partisans, and it joined a federation that included Croatia and Serbia. However, Yugoslavia's ethnic groups never forgot the massacres and betrayals that occurred during World War II. Many thousands of Serbs, Croats, and Muslims had been killed during the war, mostly at the hands of each other. In the early 1990s, demagogues from Serbia and Croatia used the atrocities that occurred during World War II to rekindle ethnic hatred in an attempt to gain support for their nationalist wars against Bosnia.

Ethnic Pride, Ethnic Hatred

J.P.

When Communism ended in Yugoslavia, the various ethnic groups living in the country enjoyed sudden freedom. With Communism's taboos against religion and ethnic pride removed, Croats, Serbs, and Muslims were able to practice their religions openly, celebrate ethnic holidays, and express their appreciation for their cultural heritage. This renewed ethnic pride and patriotism quickly led to divisiveness, however, and various separatist movements developed in the Yugoslav republics. Nationalists began to recount past atrocities committed against them and blamed the other ethnic groups for their oppression. Eventually, these ethnic differences led to wars in Croatia, Kosovo, and Bosnia.

When war erupted in Yugoslavia, many families sent their college-age children out of the country in order to give them a chance to continue their education. To help these young people, the Open Society Fund in New York established a grant program called the Open Society Institute Supplementary Grant Program for Students from the Former Yugoslavia. Over a thousand grants were eventually awarded to students throughout the world based on application essays that the students composed. The following essay recounts one student's struggle to understand the breakup of his country. J.P. describes how he learned that the ethnic and national pride he felt while living in Yugoslavia was based on the false assumption that one group of people can be superior to another.

From "War in Yugoslavia, War Within Myself," by "J.P.," in *Children of Atlantis: Voices from the Former Yugoslavia,* edited by Zdenko Lesic (New York: Central European University Press, 1995). Reprinted with the permission of the Open Society Institute.

[In 1992] the crumbling communist regime in my country was trying to tighten the belt of the Yugoslav people for the last time. My parents, who both hold doctorates, were having a hard time providing food and basic clothing for the family. Everyone had lost the grandiose ideals of working for the 'common good.' The forty-year-old machinery of the 'dictatorship of the proletariat' was facing defeat.

Cultural Renaissance

At the same time, throughout the country, there was growing appreciation of historical tradition. In Serbia, everyone was celebrating long-forgotten holidays, waving the old Serbian flags; publications and shop-windows returned to the old Cyrillic alphabet [which is used in a modified form for the Serbian language]; there was a sense of rebirth in the air. A culture that had been 'stifled for centuries' was revived in a matter of weeks. Serbia was not alone in its renaissance—people all over Yugoslavia became much more aware of their origins, customs and religion. The richness of tradition and cultural diversity could be felt everywhere.

People suddenly felt reunited, much as they did during the post Second World War euphoria, except for one thing: the sense of togetherness did not extend beyond the boundaries of one's own particular nationality or religion. Overnight Serbo-Croatian, the predominantly spoken language, became two separate languages: Serbian and Croatian. What initially seemed to be cultural appreciation and patriotism developed into a complete misunderstanding and depreciation of other cultures and then into various separatist movements. The treacheries and massacres of the Second World War, so carefully put aside by the communists, were laid bare again, for no other reason than to show how the quisling forces of each Yugoslav nation had harmed the others.

At the time I saw the situation with the same eyes as everyone around me. I simply became one of millions of Serb nationalist voices in Yugoslavia. I remembered that I had never known my grandfather—he had been hanged by the Ustashas (Croatian quislings [traitors]). I remembered being told that my family had not been allowed to take him off the gallows for four days because the Ustashas were setting an example for the rest of the village. And I resented the Croats for that.

But at the same time I knew that there was nothing intrinsically evil about the Croats, and nothing inherently altruistic about the Serbs. The Croats' reasons for hating the Serbs seemed reasonable, too. Furthermore, some of my best friends were Croats. I could not resolve the dilemma between love for my own culture and respect for cultures that differed from mine. Long before the war erupted in my homeland, there was a war going on inside my head—a war in which I was fighting myself.

Prejudices and False Beliefs

The only way to stop the war in my mind was to gain perspective. Fortunately, I was accepted at East Carolina University in the United States. After completing my fourth year of high school, I crossed the Atlantic as a seventeen-year-old with a suitcase in each hand and the desire to find answers to the questions burning within me. Living in the States for a year, I encountered entirely different cultures and outlooks. I learned that there was no single correct view of the world, no one outlook that was somehow better than others. I began to understand the subjective nature of thoughts and opinions. I saw people dealing with problems that were very different from those in my country. I started seeing the 'larger picture,' a picture where no nation is sufficient unto itself, a picture where each culture, however unique and special it may seem, is just a part of the bigger cultural mosaic of the world. This realization has helped me to resolve my own private war.

Now I know that all my justification and rationalization of the Serbian nationalist movement was irrelevant, because each claim inevitably started from a set of prejudices and beliefs that placed one people above another. Now I see that the conflict in Yugoslavia is really due to an inability to forget the past—a past that was at times certainly bloody, fraudulent and malignant. During the forty years of the 'dictatorship of the proletariat' in Yugoslavia, 'forgetting' the past was an act imposed by the rulers, not an act of the heart. The recent demise of communism in Yugoslavia released the demons of nationalism, and the inability to forgive the injustices of the past. Someone had to be blamed for the hardships of everyday life, and nothing is easier than to blame others for one's own misfortunes. The seamless mesh of these two factors, strengthened and perpetuated by gruesome media abuse, culminated in civil war. Once this was 'achieved,' even the most open-minded people took sides, blaming others for the pain of their wartime losses.

While I seem to have stopped the war inside my head, my country is still being torn apart by a senseless violence. The unspoken pain of a homeland entangled in a civil war is constantly with me. My own understanding of the issues has not helped to resolve the conflict. This is why I am eager to return home. I believe that my experience, like that of any other Yugoslav abroad, can bring understanding among the people of my country. I hope that my Bosnian, Croat and Serb brothers will soon see the futility of hatred, and realize that avenging the past will do no one any good.

The War According to Serbs

Florence Hamlish Levinsohn

When Muslim-dominated Bosnia seceded from Yugoslavia in March 1992, Bosnian Serbs suddenly found themselves an ethnic minority in the land of their birth. Fearing Muslim domination, the Serbs formed the Bosnian Serb Army (BSA) and began to invade the Muslim regions of the country, hoping to establish Serb-controlled territories. Many commentators who watched the speed with which the BSA gained control of nearly 70 percent of Bosnia argued that Serbia had to be supplying the army with arms and soldiers. As the war dragged on, the media also began to accuse the Serbs of atrocities such as torture in Serb-run concentration camps and rapes of Muslim women. The international community denounced both the Bosnian Serbs and Serbia.

In the following interview conducted by independent journalist Florence Hamlish Levinsohn, a Serb correspondent, Mirjana Kameretzy, claims that the Serbian people have been victimized throughout history. Kameretzy contends that in the Bosnian war, Bosnian Serbs were merely trying to reclaim land that had been stolen from them during Communist leader Tito's reign in Yugoslavia that began just after World War II. She argues that the international media has unfairly blamed the Serbs for the war and claims that all sides of the war committed atrocities during the conflict.

From *Belgrade: Among the Serbs*, by Florence H. Levinsohn. Copyright © 1994 by Florence Hamlish Levinsohn. Reprinted by permission of Ivan R. Dee, Publisher.

[B]elgrade correspondent for the *New York Times*] Mirjana [Kameretzy] told me she thought the world's media were not fully telling the Serb side of the story. "I think the Serb side has been ignored. I think this has happened because it's hard for people to change their focus. The story began in Slovenia when the Yugoslav army *was* the aggressor, and then in Croatia too at first. But when the story began to change, people had a hard time changing with it. People tend to get stuck with an idea. I also think Germany was pushing very hard that Yugoslavia should not continue in one piece, and its attitudes influenced the world and the press. For a long time before the war, Germany was supporting this idea and encouraging the Croatians and the Slovenians to separate. It was a terrible mistake for everyone to recognize Slovenia and Croatia, but it was what the Germans wanted. Then the same thing happened with Bosnia. People on the outside would not understand what that meant to the Serbs. The day Bosnia was recognized, the 6th of April, [1992] was the date people here remember so well. It was the Nazi bombing of Belgrade in 1941. The recognition on that day was unbelievable to the people here. For the Serbs, that day brought back all those terrible memories of World War II under the Germans."

German Interference

Why was Germany pushing for the breakup of Yugoslavia?

"I don't know. It is very difficult to understand. But it is clear that in the very near future Germany is going to be so strong they will be able to do anything they want." It was the same theory I'd heard the night before from what I'd considered two mad zealots. This woman was clearly not a zealot."

Did she think the Germans wanted to rebuild their empire?

"Well, not the way it was, but . . . you know, the Germans feel a natural affinity to the Slovenians and the Croatians. They were under the German [Austro-Hungarian] empire for so long [before World War I]. They didn't have their own country like Serbia did. They are more Germanic peoples, more industrious—you know, forget about the past, think about the future. The main character of the Serbs is to be much more involved with tradition, with their history. During the Communist regime it was not proper to think about such things, and the Serbs felt as if they had lost their identity. This is why [Serbian president Slobodan] Milosevic became so popular, because he was always speaking about the Serbs as a third nation, how they had to get their identity back."

"When I was here in 1990," I said, "just before the election, I was reading the English-language paper and found it very hard to fathom Milosevic. On one hand he was talking about maintaining Yugoslavia at all costs. And on the other he was making strong nationalist speeches filled with hate for the Croatians. But he got away with it. And people obviously loved it."

Thousands of people were displaced during the war. The tractor that brought this man and his family to safety became their temporary shelter.

Injustice Toward Serbia

"They did. The people felt that during the [regime of the Communist leader of Yugoslavia Tito] they were somehow suppressed by that regime. It was always favoring other parts of the country and not Serbia. And Serbia was the biggest republic, of course, the most numerous. Serbs felt a great deal of injustice was done to them. For instance, a great many factories were moved out of Serbia to Bosnia, Croatia, and Slovenia. Not a lot of people knew about that. I knew certain economists and so I knew about it. The explanation given, curiously, was that the parts of the country that were not devastated in the war should receive the same help as Serbia which was badly devastated and getting supposedly disproportionate assistance. So factories that had been in Serbia were just moved to other parts of the country. The explanation does not make sense. Why take factories away when you are trying to rebuild an economy? The Serbs felt it was to strip them of their power.

"It was always a mystery. You know, Croatia was not bombed by the Allies, but Belgrade and other towns in Serbia were. On Easter Day in 1944. . . .

"It was carpet bombing, and certain parts of Belgrade were completely wiped out. This was, after all, after the Nazis had already bombed us. All the smaller one-story houses in Belgrade, they don't exist anymore. And then there were several more bombings of Belgrade and then other towns in Serbia. And we were fighting on the side of the Allies! At this same time Croatia, a Nazi puppet, was never bombed. It was crazy. And no one knows why."

Muslim Executioners

Though Mirjana was disturbed that the Serbian side of the war story had not been told in the world press, she said she did not defend what she described as "the crimes that were committed in this war. I cannot defend some of the killing in Bosnia. But you have to remember that the bloodshed against the Serbs and the concentration camps for them in World War II were far worse than anything we have seen in this war. In the parts of Croatia where Serbs lived then, entire villages were destroyed. As bad as it was in Croatia, it was worse in the western part of Bosnia. The Croats called the Muslims the 'flowers of Croatia.' There were Catholics, even priests, involved, but the Muslims were the worst executioners in the concentration camps. They even had one military unit that fought with the Nazis in Stalingrad."

I was reminded of a passage in *Genocide in Satellite Croatia 1941–1945* by a French historian, Edmond Paris. He wrote: "Hatred and sadism in the form of various tortures were prevalent and cannot be compared with atrocities committed even in the darkest medieval times. The means of torture were the following: red hot needles forced under

---

Serbs Are Innocent, No Doubt

Slobodan Milosevic, president of Serbia during the war in Bosnia, has been excoriated by the international community for helping the Bosnian Serbs fight against the Muslims. Critics of Milosevic claimed that he knowingly supported ethnic cleansing, Serb-run concentration camps, and Serbian rapes of Muslim women by providing the Bosnian Serb Army with food and arms. In the following excerpt from a 1995 interview with Time *magazine, Milosevic answers his critics by claiming that Bosnia was never a legitimate nation, and his only goal in helping his fellow Serbs was to retain a united Yugoslavia.*

B osnia . . . was illegally proclaimed as an independent state and recognized [by the international community]. That recognition was like when the Roman Emperor Caligula appointed his horse as a Senator: they recognized a state that never existed before. The Serbs there said, "We want to stay within Yugoslavia. We don't want to be second-class citizens." And then the conflicts were started by Muslims, no doubt. And the Serbs, in defending themselves, were always better fighters, no doubt. And they achieved results, no doubt. But please, we [Serbs from Serbia] were insisting on peace. The international community gave premature recognition first of Slovenia and then of Croatia and supported the independence of Bosnia . . . on a totally irregular basis.

James R. Gaines et al. "Interview with Slobodan Milosevic: I Am Just an Ordinary Man," *Time*, July 17, 1995.

the finger nails; red hot irons placed between the fingers and the toes; whipping by chains; plucking out eyes; mutilating various parts of the body; placing salt in open wounds; tightening chains around the forehead until the eyes popped out and the skull was fractured; placing a person into a wire enclosure, called a hedgehog; confinement to a room filled with blood to the ankles.

"Once Bosnia declared itself a separate republic," Mirjana went on, "we all knew what would happen. There would be blood up to the knees, as we would say. And if this would come to Serbia, the blood would come up to the ears. So we knew. We knew exactly what would happen in Bosnia. We were warning the other countries about this.

"We have not understood the Allies, Europe and America. How come they are willing for the outside borders of Yugoslavia to be changed but not the inside borders, when those borders were drawn artificially?" The Yugoslav wars have been essentially about its internal borders, about the demands of the Croatians and Bosnians that they maintain the borders drawn up by Tito. These borders removed land from Serbia and followed no ethnic lines; in fact they mixed ethnic groups with the hope of making a united Yugoslavia of highly disparate peoples. The Serbs fighting in Croatia and then in Bosnia were fighting to regain old Serb lands for Serbia or to establish separate republics on land traditionally held by Serbs, such as the Krajina in Croatia.

Mirjana told me, "Actually, the Croatian policy was a shortsighted one. They could have had all the Serbs of Krajina on their plate and in twenty or thirty years they would all have been Croatians. With no war. Instead, when [Croatian president Franjo] Tudjman came to power the Cyrillic alphabet of the Serbs was not allowed. Serb newspapers and magazines could not be published. People were thrown out of their jobs. This is why they rebelled.

Prisoner-of-War Camps

"As for Bosnia, I don't agree with what they are calling concentration camps, I would call them prisoner-of-war camps.

But there are endless stories in Belgrade of people who escaped from Bosnia and the suffering they went through. There are between 700,000 and 800,000 refugees in Yugoslavia from Bosnia and Croatia. And some of them are Muslims and those who are mixed Bosnian and Serb or Croatian and Serb. It is all unbelievable. When I went to inquire about some of these people, I was given only initials. I was told I could not use their names because they still had relatives back in Bosnia. But to present this information to the UN or any of the other countries, you had to give the full names."

Had Mirjana seen the "prisoner-of-war" camps? She had not. Did she believe they were as described in the West, with people starving to death? "I can believe that," she said. "You see, Bosnia is a very mountainous country. They don't have very much food. Yugoslavia is actually shipping food to the Bosnian Serbs and to the Krajina because those people are starving. Regardless of whether they are Muslims or Serbs in Bosnia, they are really starving. What you've seen in the camps is that the Serbs are just not sharing their little bit of food with their prisoners, but they too would be starving if it weren't for the Yugoslav shipments."

Rape Fiction

What did she think about the rapes of which the Serbs were accused? "If the numbers of Serbs in Croatia and Bosnia by comparison with the Croatians and the Muslims are correct—and I have no reason to doubt the census—then the Serbs must be supermen. [Serbs are a minority in Bosnia and Croatia.] And the rapes of Serbs by the Muslims and Croatians are not even mentioned. There are some terrible stories, including some babies that have been born here in Belgrade after the women had been raped. There was a case of a mother who gave birth to a girl and refused to see the child. There are many of these stories." Mirjana told me that these stories had all been documented by the Serbian Council for Information, along with other atrocities committed against the Serbs.

"One story they're telling in the States is that Serbs are

using rape to populate Bosnia with Serbs," I said.

"That's utter nonsense. Rape is terrible, and I don't say that the Serbs didn't do it and many other things just as terrible. But their side should be published. That story is just utter nonsense invented by the Muslims."

The Yugoslav Army

"I have heard in the States that 97 or so percent of the Yugoslav budget goes to the army," I told Mirjana.

"It is 75 percent. That is to maintain the army in Yugoslavia, not to fight in Bosnia, though."

"I've also heard that 70 percent of the army is Serbian."

"You have to understand, when Yugoslavia was one nation the army consisted of people from all the republics, but the Serbs are the most numerous people, so naturally the army was mostly Serbian. [The Yugoslav army was the fourth largest in Europe, maintained because of the continuing fear of an invasion by the Soviets.] After the recognition of independence and the start of the war—I would call it a civil war really—the Serbians in the army came to Serbia, the Slovenians remained in Slovenia, the Croats in Croatia, and the Bosnians the same. Now the Yugoslav army has other nationalities as well—Russians, Hungarians, Albanians, though the Albanians are refusing to be drafted, and, of course, the Montenegrins, though there are very few of them. Their population is less than 600,000.

"But who is fighting in Bosnia is the Bosnian Serbs, supported largely by the Serb army from the Krajina, the Krajina Republican Army, because they have proclaimed their own republic, which of course has not been recognized by anyone. And then you have irregular paramilitary troops who go to fight under the Krajina army. But the regular Yugoslav army is not fighting in Bosnia."

"If the regular army is not fighting in Bosnia, why is the budget for it so massive?" I asked.

"Because it is felt that the army must be maintained at full strength in case of attack."

"I am assuming that the army can't buy any equipment or

arms now, under the embargo. I know that the Yugoslav munitions plants are in Bosnia. Are they accessible to the Serbs there so that they can get arms?"

"Well, a few are on Serb territory and a few on Croatian territory, but the majority of the munitions plants are under the control of the Muslims now."

"So the Muslims can get munitions there?"

"Well, if the plants are still operating. Nothing is really operating in Bosnia now. No, they are getting arms from the Muslim world."

Was Yugoslavia supplying arms to the Bosnian Serbs? "I would imagine some, but I don't know. But since the borders have been so dramatically closed, it may be hard. Most of what Serbia is helping the Bosnians with is food. That's why we have such a shortage of food here. I couldn't buy bread for two days now."

The War According to Croats

Warren Zimmermann

When Bosnian Serbs began the Bosnian war in the Spring of
1992, Croatia—which was also warring with Serbs—was in
alliance with Bosnia. However, Croats who lived in Bosnia
feared that the newly independent state of Bosnia—which
was dominated by Muslims—posed a threat to them. In con-
sequence, Bosnian Croats declared the Croatian independent
state of Herceg-Bosna in July 1992 and began to fight the
Muslims. Finally, in February 1994, the Bosnian government
and the Croatian Defense Council agreed on a cease-fire
accord. Bosnia's president Alija Izetbegovic and Croatia's
president Franjo Tudjman then signed an agreement to link
Bosnia and Croatia in a federation.

In the following excerpt from his book *Origins of a Catastrophe*, Warren Zimmermann recalls an interview he conducted in 1992 with Croatia's president. Zimmermann, who
served as the United States ambassador to Yugoslavia from
1989 to 1992, reports that Tudjman felt that Bosnian Muslims
wanted to transform the Balkans into an Islamic state, which
posed a threat not only to Croatia but to Europe and the
United States. Tudjman believed that Croatia and Serbia had
the right to divide Bosnia between them because Bosnia had
been artificially created by the recent Communist regime and
was not a real nation.

From *Origins of a Catastrophe*, by Warren Zimmermann. Copyright © 1996 by Warren
Zimmermann. Used by permission of Times Books, a division of Random House.

[C]roatia's president, Franjo] Tudjman as usual was more bluff in his approach to Bosnia [than was Serbia's president Slobodan Milosevic]. Among his closest advisers was his defense minister Gojko Susak, a Darth Vader-like individual with black eyebrows and a permanent scowl, whose Canadian fortune had gone into supporting Tudjman's party and, it was believed, buying arms for Croatia. Susak was originally from Herzegovina, and his foremost objective was to wrest the Croatian part of Herzegovina from Bosnia and join it to Croatia. Susak and his ilk relentlessly pressed this agenda on Tudjman, but the Croatian leader didn't need a lot of encouragement. In a long meeting with me on January 14, 1992, just a few weeks after his German protectors had bullied the European Community into supporting Bosnia's independence, Tudjman spent over an hour trying to convince me that Bosnia should be split up between Croatia and Serbia. It was the most astonishing single discussion of my years in Yugoslavia.

Islamic Bosnia

Tudjman began with a fifteen-minute monologue. He had just met with a delegation of Croats from Bosnia, who told him they felt threatened by [Bosnia's president Alija] Izetbegovic's policies. Tudjman's description of those policies was breathtaking. "The Muslims," he said, "want to establish an Islamic fundamentalist state. They plan to do this by flooding Bosnia with 500,000 Turks. Izetbegovic has also launched a demographic threat. He has a secret policy to reward large families so that in a few years the Muslims will be a majority in Bosnia [at the time they were 44 percent]. The influence of an Islamic Bosnia will then spread through the Sandzak and Kosovo [Muslim areas of Serbia] to Turkey and to Libya. Izetbegovic is just a fundamentalist front man for Turkey; together they're conspiring to create a Greater Bosnia. Catholics and Orthodox alike will be eradicated. I tell you, Mr. Ambassador, that if we in Croatia abandon the Croats in Bosnia to such a fate, they will turn on us. Some will become terrorists, and they won't spare Zagreb in their acts of revenge."

Tudjman admitted that he had discussed these fantasies with Milosevic, the Yugoslav army leadership, and the Bosnian Serbs, and "they agree that the only solution is to divide up Bosnia between Serbia and Croatia." Magnanimously, Tudjman said he didn't insist on a 50-50 division. "Let Milosevic take the larger part; he controls it anyway. We can do with less than 50 percent. We're willing to leave the Muslims a small area around Sarajevo. They may not like it, but a stable Balkans is possible only if there's a change in Bosnia's borders, no matter what the Muslims think. There's nothing sacred about those borders. Bosnia isn't an old state, like Croatia, which once extended all the way to Zemun [a western suburb of Belgrade]."

The Muslim Danger

Listening to Tudjman, I realized I had to abandon diplomatic niceties. With considerable emotion I reminded him, recalling the 1979 Iran hostage crisis [in which Iranian students seized the American embassy in Tehran and took fifty-two Americans hostage], that the United States had a lot more experience with Islamic fundamentalism than he did. In our view Izetbegovic was neither a radical fundamentalist nor a threat to anybody. The United States would strongly oppose the breakup of Bosnia. "Nobody who wants to do this can count on any assistance from us. The threat in Bosnia comes from the Serbs and the Yugoslav National Army (JNA), not from the Muslims. There will be war in Bosnia if you try to divide it. Don't you think the Muslims will react? What you propose ignores the rights of a large share of Bosnia's population."

Tudjman was unrepentant. He accused the United States of short-sightedness for not seeing the Muslim danger: "A greater Muslim state is not only a threat to Serbia and Croatia. It's also a threat to Europe and the United States." He then began, astoundingly, to defend the Serbian position on Bosnia. "The reason there's no peace there is that the Bosnian Serbs haven't been properly dealt with. New borders will solve their problems and reduce tensions." I asked, "Mr. President, how can you expect the West to help you get back the large part of Croatia taken by the Serbs when you yourself are advancing naked and unsupported claims against a neighboring republic?"

Bosnia Doesn't Really Exist

Tudjman replied that Bosnia "doesn't really exist—it was created by colonial powers and reaffirmed by communists." I told him Bosnia was as real as Croatia. Tudjman retreated to a might-makes-right argument: "If the two major groups agree, the Muslims will be compelled [to] go along." I asked, "How can you expect Milosevic to respect a deal with you to divide Bosnia when he's trying to annex part of Croatia?" Amazingly, Tudjman said about his sworn enemy, "Because I can trust Milosevic."

During this surreal discussion I could see that Tudjman's aides in the room were as flabbergasted as I was at the Croatian president's tirade against Izetbegovic and the Muslims. Several times Tudjman's chief of staff, Hrvoje Sarinic, a moderate technocrat skilled at taking the sharp edges off his boss's diatribes, tried to divert Tudjman from his multiple self-incriminations. Sarinic explained that the proposal to divide Bosnia had been Milosevic's, that he had raised it with Tudjman the week before in Brussels, and that he had claimed that Greece and France also favored the idea. Tudjman brushed off this and other efforts to rescue him from his cynical assertions. He was determined to tell me that, even as his own Croatian people were suffering the effects of a terrible war, he was ready to collude with their aggressor to carry out a similar aggression against another people.

Just before I left, I told Tudjman heatedly that, if he was trying to seek compensation in Bosnia for Serbia's incursions in Croatia, he could expect zero support from the United States. As Sarinic accompanied me down the stairs, I asked him if I had gotten too emotional in defending the integrity of Bosnia. "Oh no," he replied. "You were just fine."

This extraordinary meeting crystallized Tudjman's complicity in the violent death of Yugoslavia and the wars in Croatia and Bosnia. His toleration, even encouragement, of racist attitudes toward Serbs in Croatia made his republic undemocratic and explosive. The Krajina Serbs [who were waging war to establish a Serb-controlled region in Croatia] were militant and provocative, but Tudjman's insensitive policies only locked them into their intransigence. More than half the Serbs in Croatia didn't live in the border areas; many had Croatian spouses and were integrated into Croatian life. They too were insulted at the second-class status they were assigned.

Tudjman showed contempt for Yugoslavia and its Croatian prime minister. That was his prerogative, but when he connived with Milosevic, his implacable adversary, to divide Bosnia against the will of the Muslims and most of the Croats there, he transgressed the most basic of democratic norms. It was one thing to seek to leave Yugoslavia, quite another to take a piece out of a republic that merited the same sovereign rights as Tudjman's Croatia.

The War According to Muslims

Peter Maass

> When Bosnian Serbs gained control of nearly 70 percent of
> Bosnia in April of 1992, Bosnian Muslims banded together
> and fought back. Resisting domination was made more diffi-
> cult when Bosnia's neighbor and ally, Croatia, suddenly took
> advantage of Bosnia's weakened state and invaded the coun-
> try as well. Yet even when the international community failed
> to intervene on Bosnia's behalf, Bosnian Muslims continued
> to fight for their homeland.
>
> Peter Maass, an American foreign correspondent and staff
> writer for the *Washington Post,* learned why the Muslims
> resisted domination by speaking with his Bosnian friends.
> Maass explains that Muslims felt like Jews during World War II
> when the Nazis forced them to identify themselves as Jews, not
> Germans, and attempted to expunge them from the country.
> Using parallel logic, Maass conjectures that Americans would
> resist too if Canada and Mexico tried to exterminate them.
> Unfortunately, in banding together to fight for their country,
> many Bosnians began to embrace Muslim nationalism, which
> will destroy the multi-ethnic character of Bosnia forever.

Why didn't they just give up? It is one thing to fight on
a single front, but it is something quite different to
fight on two fronts, which is what the Bosnians had to do
when Croatia chose the Judas option [of betraying under
the guise of friendship]. Croatian President Franjo Tudj-

From *Love Thy Neighbor*, by Peter Maass. Copyright © 1996 by Peter Maass. Used by
permission of Alfred A. Knopf, a division of Random House, Inc.

man, whose appetite for a chunk of Bosnia was well-known but unsated, gave his forces a green light to conquer as much of Bosnia as they could manage. The trickle of food and weapons that had sustained Bosnia in the war's first year came through Croatia, and this lifeline was severed when Croats' first mortar was fired at Bosnia. A year after the Serbs began cleansing and killing Muslims, Croats began doing the same thing, like the vulture after the predator. Extinction beckoned.

Conquer and Cleanse

In America, we have a hard time understanding why people in places like Bosnia are willing to suffer so much in a futile war. The goal of imperial wars, which we are most familiar with, is to conquer and rule. The goal of nationalist wars, as in Bosnia, is to conquer and cleanse. These contests are winner-take-all. When you are faced with enemies who wish to expunge you from your land, and when those enemies offer a treaty that ensures their boots will stay on your throat, suffocating you one day, you have little choice but to keep struggling, even though the odds are against you and people who call themselves your friends are saying you should give up. Resistance becomes not an option but an imperative.

Emir Tica taught me the meaning of resistance. Emir was one of those Bosnians whom I only met a few times but cannot forget, and somehow consider a friend. He was in his early thirties, well under six feet tall, and had brown hair and blue eyes. He liked heavy metal. Emir lived in Travnik, an ancient, minaret-filled town that was a regional capital during the Ottoman empire, and the birthplace of Ivo Andric, the famed writer. Emir worked as an adjutant to Travnik's commander, and because Emir spoke English well, he also served as an unofficial liaison with foreign journalists, which is why our paths crossed.

"It is becoming clear to me that we are completely alone," Emir said at army headquarters, a restaurant where a guard at the door was equipped with a laughably outdated Tommy gun. "We as a people are in danger of simply disappearing.

I have never called myself a Muslim, but now I must feel like a Muslim, because European Muslims are faced with obliteration. I know history, from books and movies, and I know that in the Nazi times they tried to destroy a people, the Jews. We are now starting to feel like the Jews must have felt in 1940, when they realized it was for real. But we must survive, at least two of us. It is not a question of who will survive but that someone must survive. In order to kill a people, you must kill memory, you must destroy everything that belongs to that people. But if two people can stay alive, they can remember. The Jews can remember, and I expect they can understand what is happening here better than anyone else."

Dark Forces of History

It was hard to escape the Jewish analogy, and perhaps that's why I found my travels in Bosnia to be increasingly depressing. My ancestors would have liked to consider themselves Germans, or German Jews, but in the end they were

Serbs Lit the Fire

Under the communist regime of Josip Broz, known as Tito, the republics and provinces of Yugoslavia became united and enjoyed relatively prosperous times. When Tito died in 1980, however, the ethnic tensions that had been suppressed under his reign resurfaced. Nationalistic movements in several of the republics including Croatia and Bosnia were denounced by Serbia, which wanted to retain a united Yugoslavia. In the following 2000 interview with theology professor Stephen J. Pope, Father Ivo Markovic, a Bosnian Croat who worked for multicultural peace in Bosnia, argues that Serbia started the war. He claims that the Serbs used propaganda to make Yugoslav Christians believe that Bosnian Muslims were a threat to them.

Over 15 or 20 years ago we [in Yugoslavia] had a feeling that the end of Communism was coming. . . . We were

Jews, just Jews, not Germans at all, and they had to leave or die. Emir had made the same mistake. He thought he was a Bosnian, or a Bosnian Muslim, but in the end he was a Muslim, just a Muslim, and other people, stronger ones, wanted his land and were willing to kill him for it. The same dark forces of history were at work, although this time the victims had a better opportunity to resist, and so, even on two fronts, they resisted.

What's surprising is the fact that presidents and prime ministers in the West were surprised at Bosnia's stubbornness. It is entirely natural for a people to continue fighting for their land or freedom until they are no longer capable of fighting. Let me suggest an approximate parallel. Imagine, for a moment, that Mexico and Canada mounted a surprise attack and gained control of two-thirds of America, cleansing the conquered territory. The bulk of the population is crammed into the Midwest, the only land still held by our government. The West Coast and East Coast are occupied by the enemy. Would we agree to a peace treaty that gave

---

happy that Communism was going to end, but we also knew that [Yugoslav leader] Marshall Tito's powerful bureaucracy would not dissolve quietly. While we saw that the situation was one of terrible danger, I believed, wrongly, that we would be able to avoid a real catastrophe. The problem was that the Communists would never allow problems to surface. They always pushed them under the rug. But in 1988 the problems came to public light. At the outset, [Serbian President] Slobodan Milosevic and the Serbs lit the fire. They justified it by a propaganda campaign that created massive fear. They made people think that Christians were being attacked by Muslims. In 1992 Serbs attacked Croats and Muslims. At first the Croats and Muslims joined together against the Serbs, but then Franjo Tudjman, the president of Croatia, decided to take the Croats to war against the Muslims.

Stephen J. Pope, "Making Peace After Catastrophe: An Interview with Ivo Markovic," *America*, September 23, 2000.

most of the country to the Canadians and Mexicans, leaving us sandwiched between them, at their mercy for supplies? Remember, tens of thousands of our men have been tortured and killed by the Canadians and Mexicans, and tens of thousands of our women have been raped. The question is a no-brainer; we would continue fighting until we won back our land or were driven into the Grand Canyon.

In such situations, you fight in whatever way you can, with whatever weapons you have. When the Croats attacked, completely shutting off the Bosnian Army from outside supplies, the Bosnians survived by improvisation. If the terrain was appropriate, explosives were packed into barrels and rolled downhill at the enemy. These were known as barrel bombs. When the Bosnians ran out of artillery casings, they stuffed explosives into fire extinguishers. They even turned soda pop cans into mortar shells and grenades. They were one step away from reverting to impalings. And it worked. They held off the Croats, who, a year later, called off their failed offensive and patched up their alliance with the Bosnians.

Muslim Nationalism

Just as resistance is natural in situations like that, so, unfortunately, is radicalization. Feeling betrayed by America and Europe, the Muslim leadership in Bosnia began turning away from Western notions of pluralism, and focused on Muslim nationalism. It was the cruelest of self-fulfilling prophecies: The Western world viewed them as Muslims, not Europeans, so they became Muslims, tough Muslims. They had little choice—with the United Nations as global cop, the meek shall not inherit the earth. . . .

When they started the war, Serbs claimed that Muslims wanted to set up an Islamic state. It was nonsense, of course, and it still is. But what's true is that Bosnia's multinational society has been eroded by the corrosive effects of the long war; virtue is degraded rather than rewarded in protracted military conflicts. A year after the war started, well-educated liberals with connections outside Bosnia began leaving in greater numbers, thereby letting less tolerant militants get a stronger grip on the hearts and minds of those who remained behind. This is perhaps the saddest part of Bosnia's tragedy, that its unique mosaic of nationalities, held together by civic tolerance, may disappear forever even in cities controlled by the government. With luck, Emir and those who share his views might triumph, not only against Serb and Croat nationalists, but against Muslim nationalists, too. My hopes are with Emir, but I am not hopeful. It would be a true pity for Bosnia, which has lost so many lives already, to lose its soul.

"I don't want to live in an Islamic country," Emir said. "I drink alcohol. I don't pray or go to a mosque. When I listen to music, I listen to Guns N' Roses, Neil Young, AC/DC. When I read books, I read Mark Twain. When I speak a foreign language, it is English. I don't know how to speak Arabic. My country is Bosnia, and Bosnia exists only with all its nationalities. I don't want to live with only Muslims. Can you imagine living in California with only white people?"

Chapter 2

Atrocities

Chapter Preface

Namka Hedis watched as Serbian soldiers called Chet-niks shot her husband in front of her house. Then the Chetniks put a knife to her throat, pointed at her four children, and said, "Choose which one of your children is to die. You must give us one of them." According to journalist Paul Harris—who interviewed Namka after the event—the aggrieved mother could not choose which child to sacrifice, so the soldiers seized her youngest daughter, Anita. Although the Chetniks did not kill Anita, the child was so traumatized by what occurred that day she no longer speaks. The Serbian soldiers then turned the family out of the village, forcing them to become refugees.

Ethnic cleansing—a term coined for the type of genocide engaged in during the Bosnian war—took many forms. In most cases, invading soldiers such as the Chetniks rounded up the men in the village and murdered them on the spot. Sometimes the men were sent to prisoner-of-war camps where they were tortured and eventually murdered. Muslim women were often raped and then killed. Victims of ethnic cleansing who were not killed became refugees, many of whom have remained displaced after the war. It is estimated that the Balkan wars that began in 1991 created the largest refugee population in Europe since the Second World War. Most refugees cannot return home. Namka's village, for example, was completely erased by the Chetniks.

The ultimate goal of all ethnic cleansing is to remove a population in order to free up the region for occupation by the conquering people. The Bosnian Serb pogrom was successful in that it resulted in the establishment of a Serb republic within Bosnia. However, refugees like Namka who were cleansed from the area suffer emotional problems long after the victors have celebrated their territorial gains.

Massacre at Stupni Do

Anthony Loyd

> The war in Bosnia was at times fought on two fronts: With
> Serbia to the east and with Croatia to the west. When
> Bosnia's war with Serbia began in the Spring of 1992, Bosnia
> was in alliance with Croatia. This alliance was short-lived,
> however, and in the summer of that year, Croatia began to
> invade parts of Bosnia. In an attempt to create a Croatian state
> within Bosnia, the Bosnian Croat Army began to destroy
> Bosnian villages and murder the Muslim inhabitants, a
> process called ethnic cleansing. Croatia's attempts to wrest
> control of regions in Bosnia quickly failed, however, and in
> the Spring of 1994, the Croats once again formed an alliance
> with Bosnia.
>
> At the height of Croatia's campaign against the Muslims in
> 1993, independent British journalist and photographer
> Anthony Loyd traveled throughout central Bosnia and wit-
> nessed the destruction of several Muslim villages. In the fol-
> lowing excerpt from his book, *My War Gone By, I Miss It So*,
> Loyd describes the massacre at Stupni Do. After viewing the
> charred buildings and the mutilated bodies of the villagers,
> Loyd comes to understand the hunger for retribution.

Stupni Do—a whirlpool black and white transparency that
sucked the colour out of your mind and eyes. The village
blown to rubble-strewn shreds. Livestock roasted in the char-
coal stalls of their stables. Humans smashed and burned. Not

From *My War Gone By, I Miss It So*, by Anthony Loyd. Copyright © 1999 by Anthony
Loyd. Reprinted by permission of Grove/Atlantic, Inc. and Transworld Publishers Ltd.

a sign of life. Even a child's rabbit crushed like a bloody white cloth in the dust. The raised houses like crematorium where the dead spat and crackled beneath the heat of torched masonry. Swedish soldiers [from the United Nations] standing mute with shock. A captain shaking with rage: 'This is fucking shit, this is worse than fucking shit, this is . . .' The words just gagged to a choke in the back of his throat. There were no words to describe this. A body no bigger than a black carrier bag cocktail-sticked by white tibia. Another half fried. Its head smashed in. Face-down. A child. And what do you say? Fuck fuck fuck fuck and Jesus fucking Christ. It's not enough and the rage comes in like a hurricane and then you want them dead, the people who did this, you want the scum erased for this. You could do it yourself there and then at that moment, blast every one of them forward in a pink spray. And walk away to find some more.

The Open Scar

And there was something more than what you saw, smelled and felt inside. The atmosphere. It chainsawed through your senses and squirmed glass over your body; shut your eyes and you could still hear the screaming. For whatever had been sucked out of that place, something else had been pumped in. An open scar in the ether; pleading chokes scabbing the edges. Some empty black infinity inside that spat and laughed. Ever had a bad hallucination? You've seen nothing. Nothing.

Only one room in that place was untouched by flame. It was no more than a stone-floored shed, tacked to the wall of a burned house at the far end of the village. The light was fading fast grey-black and the Swedes had gone and the mist came rolling in tendril waves down through the forest into the ruins and I knew that whatever it was that made me want to run up the track back to the Land-Rovers and out of it had nothing to do with the threat of the Bosnian Croat Army (HVO) coming back. The six of us were alone. Then Kurt [an American journalist] staggered backwards out of that room he'd found, cursing and shocked, so I walked in.

The Women

For a moment I could see nothing in the smoky gloom. My torch began to flicker, dimmed and died. I beat it back into life on my thigh and looked again. Three women looked back at me.

They were kneeling in a small box-shaped pit sunk into the stone floor, huddled together in fear, their arms and hands entwined in support. Normally the hole would have

Ethnic Cleansing Works Both Ways

The international community has condemned Bosnian Serbs for the war crimes that they committed against the Muslims and, to a lesser extent the Croats, during the Bosnian war. But not all Bosnian Serbs joined the war effort on behalf of the Bosnian Serb Army or became involved in ethnic cleansing. Many Serbs remained loyal to the Bosnian government. However, as atrocities at the hands of their fellow Serbs mounted, loyal Serbs found themselves viewed as only Serbian by their neighbors and treated with disrespect or, in some cases, open hostility.

In the following excerpt from her article, "Peace Has Come to Bosnia But Hatred Has Not Gone Away," journalist Neely Tucker recounts an interview she conducted with a loyal Serb family from Zivinica. When Muslim refugees, who had been cleansed by the Bosnian Serb Army from a nearby city, fled to Zivinica in the summer of 1995, they were angered to find Serbs living in the region and threatened the Dragivic family with death. Tucker's account illustrates how ethnic hatred deepened on all sides of the conflict as the Bosnian war wore on.

There are at least 2.5 million people who have been "ethnically cleansed" from their homes in Bosnia, and the vast majority have fled elsewhere in the country. Like every reporter here, I have talked to several hundred of them—Muslims, Croats, Serbs.

been used to store grain and covered with the wooden trap-door that now lay upright on its hinges behind their backs. It would have been the ideal place to hide. Close the lid and the pit would be nearly invisible. There would have been just enough room for three people to lie beneath it. What gave them away? I wondered. A cough? A sob?

Two of the women were in their twenties, the third was an old lady. Someone had shot her in the mouth and her shattered dentures cascaded with her own teeth down her

---

The stories are depressingly familiar. After a while, you can pretty much fill in the blanks.

Last week, I was climbing yet another dilapidated stair-case in yet another run-down hotel turned over to refugees.

The hotel, this time, is the Konjuh. The town is Zivinica, in north-central Bosnia. The refugees are retired Serb coal miners who remained loyal to the Bosnian government.

Their loyalty didn't count for much when the Srbrenica refugees came to town this summer.

Srbrenica was a Muslim enclave in eastern Bosnia. Serb forces overran the U.N. protected area on July 6, [1995]. More than 6,000 Muslim men were butchered and dumped in mass graves.

When Muslim survivors reached Zivinica, they were furious to see ethnic Serbs, even if they were allies.

"Three men in uniforms came to my door with automatic rifles, grenades, knives," says Vlacko Dragivic, 61. "The lead guy slapped me. His men destroyed things in the hallway. They cursed me, they talked about my Serb mother. The lead one said they would slaughter us if we did not leave."

He and his family wound up on the fourth floor of this hotel, with its peeling brown wallpaper and stinking toilets, with about 50 other Serb families who were also expelled.

One of the old women in the room begins crying, but there is a resigned air to the afternoon. At this late date in the war, even they can't get worked up about their plight anymore.

Neely Tucker, "Peace Has Come to Bosnia But the Hatred Has Not Gone Away: A Personal Look at the War-Torn Area." *Knight-Ridder/Tribune News Service,* 1995.

front like mashed melon pips. One girl had been shot repeatedly in the chest. It was difficult to tell whether the other had had her throat cut or been shot; a great gash of blood crescented her neck. The expression on their faces had survived the damage. It was so clear. A time-valve that opened directly on to those last moments. So you saw what they saw. I hope beyond hope that I never see it again.

The Cow

In the recess of the shed something moved. It was a cow. The only survivor in Stupni Do. Someone had pulled a large plastic barrel over its head. The neck of the barrel fitted tightly around that of the beast, whose horns impaled the sides, keeping it locked in place. It must have taken a great amount of time and energy to bring the cow to this state: unable to see or eat.

So that was how we spent our last few minutes in the dusk at Stupni Do. Fighting the impulse that wanted our legs to kick us out of that place as fast and far away as possible, wrestling in a shed with a cow and a plastic barrel watched by three murdered women. Pulling and shouting and cursing and grunting with a torch that barely worked and a pathetic penknife because we wanted the cow to live. We wanted the cow to be able to see and eat again. We wanted that more than anything.

The Presence

We had seen many more bodies than those in that village. We had seen worse mutilation. It was not the dead that affected us. It was what else still lay in the place. The presence of Corinne [a photographer] seemed the only one of us to be wholly unaffected. I hope she left her cameras outside her room that night because, given what they must have filtered off before it reached her consciousness, they were surely crackling with possession.

Stupni Do was transformed the next day. Its secret out, the HVO checkpoints in the forest all but disappeared and the village was swamped by UN soldiers, European Union

(EU) monitors, war crimes investigators and journalists. Even then it preserved something of the previous day's evil. I think they finally discovered sixty bodies or so. More must have been burned to powder-ash in the houses. A British brigadier, chief of staff to the UN in Bosnia and conditioned to restraint and reserve, came out of the shed in fury having seen the three women.

'In thirty years of soldiering I have never seen the like of what I have seen here,' he declared before television cameras. 'We know who did this, Kresimir Bozic and the Bobovac Brigade and they are scum.' It was good to see a man like him so angry. If his fury managed to shatter the self-control of an officer of so many years standing, then my own reaction was more understandable. Whatever your character or the degree of your self-possession you could not escape it: a terrible deed had been committed there. Its legacy remained and would affect you deeply.

Yet we were outsiders. For Bosnians who had lost family or friends in such a way, whether it was Stupni Do or Uzdol, the hunger for retribution would be all the stronger and less easily assuaged. What we had seen that day was just the tiniest fraction of what was going on in the surrounding hills and forests. The key to our reaction lay not in feeling anger, but in the understanding it brought of how easily such atrocities provoked a response in kind. To see the vision in those three women's eyes was to see your understanding of humanity banished to a barren wilderness of darkness and howling. If you did not feel that way, then you were already there.

Rape as a Weapon of War

Roy Gutman

When the Bosnian Serb Army invaded areas of Bosnia from 1992 to 1995, it expunged most of the regions' Muslim inhabitants. This process of ethnic cleansing was an attempt to establish a Serb-only nation out of land wrested from Bosnia. Muslim men who were not killed were usually sent to concentration camps while Muslim women were often held in makeshift bordellos where they were raped, often repeatedly, by Serbian soldiers.

In the following excerpt from his book, *A Witness to Genocide*, based on his Pulitzer Prize-winning dispatches on the Bosnian war, American journalist Roy Gutman interviews some of these Muslim rape victims. Gutman learns that Serb soldiers were ordered to rape the women in order to shame and insult them.

S erb forces in northern Bosnia systematically raped 40 young Muslim women of a town they captured early [in the summer of 1992], telling some of their victims they were under orders to do so, the young women say. Statements by victims of the assault, describing their ordeal in chilling detail, bear out reports that the Serb conquerors of Bosnia have raped Muslim women, not as a by-product of the war but as a principal tactic of the war.

Reprinted with permission from Scribner's, a division of Simon & Schuster, Inc., from *A Witness to Genocide,* by Roy Gutman. Copyright © 1993 by Roy Gutman.

Orders to Rape

"'We have orders to rape the girls,'" Mirsada, 23, one of 20 young victims interviewed by *Newsday,* said the young man who abducted her told her. He said he was "ashamed to be a Serb" and added that "everything that is going on is a war crime," she said.

Hafiza, also 23, said she sought to dissuade the soldier who raped her. "I tried crying and begging," she said. "I said, 'You have a mother and a sister, a female in the family.' He said nothing. He didn't want to talk. Then he said, 'I must. I must.' I said, 'You must not if you don't want to.'" But she was unable to stop him.

The incident involved 40 young women from Brezovo Polje, a small town on the Sava River where conquering forces marched in, seized all the civilians and dispatched them according to age and gender to their assigned fate.

The rape victims were interviewed in a refugee center, their only haven after the destruction of their homes, their families and the basis of their economic survival. They agreed to be quoted and photographed provided they were identified only by first name and age.

"We want the world to know about our truth. All mothers. All women," said Senada, 17, who wrote a statement by hand and gave it to the chief gynecologist at Tuzla Hospital with the request that she pass it on to *Newsday.* "I wouldn't want anyone else to have the same experience. It is worse than any other punishment in the world."

Systematized Rape

The Brezovo Polje episode is only one of a number of indications of a pattern of systematized rape during the Serb conquest of Bosnia. In separate interviews in Tuzla, four young women from the village of Liplje, near Zvornik, said their Serb captors had detained them in a makeshift bordello where three or more men raped them every night for 10 nights. A leading Bosnian women's group has charged that upward of 10,000 Bosnian women are currently being held in Serb detention camps where their captors rape them repeatedly, although that has not been independently confirmed. Another pattern is the rape of pregnant women and some middle-aged women.

Dr. Melika Kreitmayer, leader of the gynecological team that examined 25 of the 40 victims from Brezovo Polje, said she and her colleagues are convinced that the object of the rapes was "to humiliate Muslim women, to insult them, to destroy their persons and to cause shock. . . . These women were raped not because it was the male instinct. They were raped because it was the goal of the war," she said. "My impression is that someone had an order to rape the girls." She cited as proof that some young women said they had been taken to a house and not raped but were instructed to tell others that they had been raped.

Kreitmayer, who is of Muslim origin and whose team includes a Serb and a Slovene doctor, made those assertions without any sign of objection from her colleagues. "We are shocked by what we have heard," commented her Serb colleague, Dr. Nenad Trifkovic.

According to the young women, the rapists discussed the assaults with their victims as a mission they had to accom-

During the course of the war, the Bosnian Serb Army used systemized rape as a way to demoralize Muslims.

plish. Many of the men fortified their resolve by taking white pills that appeared to stimulate them, the women said. The men's claim that they were operating under orders was reinforced when a new group of irregular forces arrived that owed its allegiance to one of the most savage of the warlords, Vojislav Seselj, a militant nationalist from Sarajevo. The leaders of the original group tried to protect the women of Brezovo Polje from the Seselj followers, the women indicated.

"'Don't worry. The girls have been raped once,'" Zlata, 23, recalled one of the officers telling the Seselj followers.

Ethnic Cleansing

According to the victims, preparations for the mass rape began early on the morning of June 17 when Serb soldiers in army uniforms and masks piled out of their minivans and rounded up the Muslims of Brezovo Polje for ethnic cleansing. They loaded the able-bodied men from 18 to 60 onto buses and sent them for interrogation to Luka, a notorious Serb-run detention camp in nearby Brcko where nine in 10 prisoners were slaughtered, according to a survivor interviewed by *Newsday*.

Then they packed about 1,000 women, children and old people into eight buses, drove them around the countryside for two days and held them under armed guard for four terrifying nights without food or water in a parking lot in the nearby town of Ban Brdo, the victims said. Serb soldiers returning from the front invaded the buses every night and led off women and girls to an unknown location at knife-point, recalled Senada, 17. "They threw them out in the morning, and their clothes were torn, and they were covered with blood," she said.

Finally the group arrived in Caparde, where about 50 Serb irregulars, bearded followers of a warlord named Zeljko Arkan, robbed the mothers and forcibly separated them from their daughters. The mothers were taken by bus and deposited in a war zone. Meanwhile, in the Osnovo furniture warehouse in Caparde, where the daughters were held, the men, mostly with long beards in the style of the World War

II Serbian royalist force known as the Chetniks, selected what one of the rapists said were the 40 prettiest young women of Brezovo Polje and raped them in groups of 10.

Hejira, 21, said she asked Dragan, the man who raped her, why they were doing it. "He said we were the cleanest convoy that passed Caparde, the prettiest and most attractive, and that they couldn't let us pass because we were so beautiful." The victims were ages 15 to 30, with wholesome looks, careful dress and gentle manners.

"They would come by and tap us on the shoulder," re-

A Means to Greater Serbia

When reports of systematic rape of Muslim women by Bosnian Serbs reached the international community, journalists flocked to Bosnian refugee camps for interviews, asking, "Anyone who was raped and speaks English?" But the majority of the women refused to talk about their experiences. For many, this refusal stemmed from a dread of exposing themselves to humiliation. Coming from a patriarchal society, these women believed that their worth was tied to their sexual purity and their ability to produce Muslim children. Rape—which often resulted in impregnation by Serbs—destroyed their identities.

In the following excerpt, taken from her article, "Women Hide Behind a Wall of Silence," New York journalist and resident of Croatia Slavenka Draculic explains how rape has historically been used as an instrument of war, and how the rapes in Bosnia differed in significant aspects from other wartime rapes.

As Susan Brownmiller and other feminists have pointed out, women have been raped in every war: as retaliation, to damage another man's "property," to send a message to the enemy. Rape is an instrument of war, a very efficient weapon for demoralization and humiliation. In World War II, Russian and Jewish women were raped by Nazis, and Soviet soldiers raped German women by the hundreds of thousands. Chinese women were raped by the Japanese, Viet-

called Hejira. "They told everyone else that we had gone to 'fetch water.' Some of the girls came back two hours later. Some the next morning. And each of them sat down and cried," she said.

The mothers arrived in Tuzla on June 23, distraught about their missing daughters and traumatized by the journey, which began with another bus ride and ended with a forced 12-mile walk through a war zone on a road littered with human corpses and animal carcasses. Their daughters arrived four days later, after a forced walk across a mined road with

namese by Americans. What seems to be unprecedented about the rapes of Muslim women in Bosnia (and, to a lesser extent, the Croat women too) is that there is a clear political purpose behind the practice. The rapes in Bosnia are not only a standard tactic of war, they are an organized and systematic attempt to cleanse (to move, resettle, exile) the Muslim population from certain territories. Serbs want to conquer in order to establish a Greater Serbia. The eyewitness accounts and reports state that women are raped everywhere and at all times, and victims are of all ages, from six to eighty. They are also deliberately impregnated in great numbers, held captive and released only after abortion becomes impossible. This is so they will "give birth to little Chetniks," the women are told. While Muslim men are killed fighting or are exterminated in about one hundred concentration camps, women are raped and impregnated and expelled from their country. Thus not only is their cultural and religious integrity destroyed but the reproductive potential of the whole nation is threatened. Of course, Croats and Muslims have raped Serbian women in Bosnia too, but the Serbs are the aggressors, bent on taking over two-thirds of the territory. This does not justify Croat and Muslim offenses, but they are in a defensive war and do not practice systematic and organized rape.

Slavenka Draculic, "Women Hide Behind a Wall of Silence," *Why Bosnia? Writings on the Balkan War.* Ed. by Rabia Ali and Lawrence Lifschultz. Stony Creek, CT: Pamphleteers Press, 1993.

several elderly people, a number of whom died en route, they said.

The young women were exhausted and in a state of shock, doctors said. Most, according to the gynecological team that later examined them, had vaginal infections of staphylococcus and other bacteria that originate in dirt or fecal matter. Almost every one of the 20 women interviewed by *Newsday* reported that the men who raped them were filthy and smelly, and in some cases had blood on their bodies.

Losing Everything

The health and psychological stresses on the young women of Brezovo Polje are only part of their tragedy, for each is missing a father or a brother as well as the material basis of their lives. They are women in the prime of life, but few have anywhere to go; and the rapes have shaken their confidence. Almost every one broke into tears as she talked over several days to this reporter.

Their trauma is not over, for as Kreitmayer noted, many of them may become pregnant. The hospital will provide hormonal drugs to induce abortion, she added.

The deepest hurt seems to be moral shame. These women were from the countryside where premarital sex is prohibited, and Kreitmayer confirmed that all but one had been virgins at the time they were raped. Most of them think they have been ruined for life.

"We all feel that we lost everything," said Heira, 25. "We have been abandoned. We have been imperiled. Every woman, if she is raped, has to feel the same."

Satka, 20, said she despised the man who raped her "because he had no feeling for me. I wasn't his girlfriend. It was savagery." She said she felt shame because "I was an honest girl. I was a virgin. I gave it to someone who didn't deserve it. Someone whom I love deserves it. But not a savage."

Meira, 17, said the man who raped her threatened her with a hand grenade. "Mine put a grenade in my hand. He told me, 'All Serbs are good, and I am a good Serb.' And if I didn't agree, he could kill both of us with a bomb." The young man took the grenade back and put it on the table. Meira said she assumed he was ordered to rape her. He did not apologize "but said that he had to do it. He said it was better for me that he did it than the followers of Seselj, who would rape 10 men to one woman."

Shame and Anger

No such excuse seemed to be forthcoming in the rape of several pregnant women, who were so shattered that they asked to have their babies aborted.

Kreitmayer said one nurse from Brezovo Polje had lost her mother, father, husband, and 4-year-old child "in front of her eyes." The woman told doctors the Serb conquerors decided not to kill her but brought her to their military hospital. "She worked every day for them, but every night she was raped. She was sick. She was desperate. She told them she was between two and three months pregnant. But it meant nothing to them," Kreitmayer said. The woman came to the gynecological clinic "so sick that she desperately wanted an abortion," the doctor said.

For the young women of Brezovo Polje, shame alternates with anger. Each time this reporter returned to the school where they are living, a larger group of victims decided to join in the discussion. Rape had been so rare over the years in Bosnia that there are few professional counselors, and Kreitmayer said this was the first appearance of mass rape and aggression toward women.

The victims say that right now they would like to be anywhere but in Bosnia. Most say that once they leave here, they do not plan to return ever again.

The White House

Rezak Hukanović

Bosnian Serbs established prisoner-of-war camps to house the Muslims and Croats they expelled from cities such as Prijedor that had been conquered by the Bosnian Serb Army. The international media began to publish reports about these camps, claiming that torture and killings were routine. Rezak Hukanović, a Bosnian radio announcer, journalist, and poet was ousted from his home in Prijedor in 1992 and sent to the Omarska prisoner-of-war camp. In the following account, which Hukanović writes in the third-person in order to convey the macabre aspect of his experience, he describes his torture at the hands of Serb guards in the building called The White House. Hukanović was eventually released from the prison camp Manjaca and fled to Norway.

Wednesday, June 10, [1992], early evening. The interrogators had already left for the day, in the van that took them back and forth from Prijedor [in Northern Bosnia]. One of the guards [of the concentration camp], drunker than usual, stuck his unkempt head through the door of the dorm and called for Djemo.

Daddy Will Be Back

The same deathly silence that accompanied night calls descended on the dorm. Djemo felt a booming in his head, as if hundreds of hammers were pounding at his temples, at the top of his skull and the nape of his neck. His heart started pounding wildly; he could feel it beating in every part of his

From *The Tenth Circle of Hell: A Memoir of Life in the Death Camps of Bosnia*, by Rezak Hukanović, translated by Colleen London and Midhat Ridjanović. Copyright © 1993 by Rezak Hukanović. Originally published in 1993 by Sypress Forlag, Oslo. English translation copyright © 1996 by BasicBooks, a division of HarperCollins Publishers, Inc. Reprinted by permission of Basic Books, a member of Perseus Books, L.L.C.

body. His blood pulsed through the labyrinth of capillaries across his face. He turned to his son and began to speak, his voice breaking: "Don't be scared, son, nothing will happen to me." Djemo hugged Ari tightly, feeling the delicate, rhythmic trembling of his fragile body.

"Ari, son, Daddy will be back, believe me." Timidly he took his son's arms off his shoulders, turned aside so that Ari wouldn't see the tears trickling down his cheeks, and started to walk away, not believing his own words. Somewhere at the back of his head he could almost feel the eyes of the poor souls whose silence spoke so eloquently. Gasps and deep sobs began from where he had been sitting, first softly, then louder and louder. Ari was weeping as the weak arms of those nearby reached out to keep him from going after his father. "Daddy, come back, please!" Djemo stopped for a second as his eyes tracked his son's voice. Something big and heavy, like a cannonball, lodged in his throat. He could hardly breathe. The tears that had trickled down his cheeks now flowed freely. Trying to flee such a merciless fate, he forced himself to utter: "I'll be back, son, I'll be back." Then he stepped forward past the guard, whose bearded face was flushed and whose eyes transmitted only darkness.

"In front of me," the guard ordered, pointing to the White House [where prisoners were routinely beaten]. On the way over he ranted and raved, cursing and occasionally pounding Djemo on the back with his truncheon. The hot, heavy air made everything even more unbearable. Djemo cast one more dull glance backward, into the distance, almost stopping. The guard pushed the barrel of his rifle hard into Djemo's back, until he felt a sharp pain and beads of sweat gathered on his face.

An overwhelming desire came over Djemo. He was on the verge of turning to spit in the bearded creature's face and punch him right in the middle of his ugly, drunken snout. But no—the voice of his son resounded in his ears like a seal ripped open within his torn heart. Defiantly, Djemo raised his head high above his shoulders and kept walking.

The guard took him to the White House, to the second room on the left. (There were no prisoners in the White House then; they were only brought in later.) The next second, something heavy was let loose from above, from the sky, and knocked Djemo over the head. He fell.

An Ancient Devil

Something flashed across his eyes, and everything became blurry. Blistering heat scorched his face and neck. He couldn't open his eyes. Half-conscious, sensing that he had to fight to survive, he wiped the blood from his eyes and forehead and raised his head. He saw four creatures, completely drunk, like a pack of starving wolves, with clubs in their hands and unadorned hatred in their eyes. Among them was the frenzied leader of the bloodthirsty pack, Zoran Zigic, the infamous Ziga whose soul, if he had one at all, was spattered with blood. He was said to have killed over two hundred people, including many children, in the "cleansing" operations around Prijedor. He took barely enough time between slaughters to put his bloody knife back into its sheath. Scrawny and long-legged, with a big black scar on his face, Ziga seemed like an ancient devil come to visit a time as cruel as his own. Anyone who came close to him also came close to death.

"Now, then, let me show you how Ziga does it," he said, ordering Djemo to kneel down in the corner by the radiator, "on all fours, just like a dog." The maniac grinned. Djemo knelt down and leaned forward on his hands, feeling humiliated and as helpless as a newborn. Just then they brought three more prisoners in from his dorm: Asaf, Kiki, and Bego. Being the last, Bego was immediately taken to the room across the way by Nikica, the youngest of the group of murderers. The sounds of beating and screaming soon reached the room Djemo was in. Asaf had to take the same position as Djemo, only at the other end of the radiator.

The tallest of the guards, another local murderer, named Duca, ordered Kiki to lie down on his back in the middle of the room. Then he jumped as high as he could and, with all his 250-odd pounds, came crashing down on Kiki's stomach and ribs. Another wild man wearing a headband came up to Asaf and started hitting him with a truncheon made out of thick electrical cable. Ziga kept hitting Djemo the whole time on the back and head with a club that unfurled itself every time he swung it to reveal a metal ball on the end. Djemo curled up, trying to protect his head by pulling it in toward his shoulders and covering it with his right hand. Ziga just kept cursing as he hit, his eyes inflamed by more and more hatred. The first drops of blood appeared on the tiles under Djemo's head, becoming denser and denser until they formed a thick, dark red puddle. Ziga kept at it; he stopped only every now and then, exhausted by his nonstop orgy of violence, to fan himself, waving his shirttail in front of his contorted face.

At some point a man in fatigues appeared at the door. It was Saponja, a member of the famous Bosna-montaza soccer club from Prijedor; Djemo had once known him quite well. He came up to Djemo and said, "Well, well, my old pal Djemo. While I was fighting in Pakrac and Lipik, you were pouring down the cold ones in Prijedor." He kicked Djemo right in the face with his boot. Then he kicked him again in the chest, so badly that Djemo felt like his ribs had been shattered by the weight of the heavy combat boots. He barely managed to stay up on his arms and legs, to keep himself from falling. He knew that if he fell it would be all over. Ziga laughed like a maniac. Then he pushed Saponja away and started hitting Djemo again with his weird club, even more fiercely than before.

Enraged Beasts

The strange smell of blood, sweat, and wailing that enveloped the room only increased the cruelty of the enraged beasts. Djemo received another, even stronger kick to the face. He clutched himself in pain, bent a little to one side, and collapsed, his head sinking into the now-sizable pool of blood beneath him. Ziga grabbed him by the hair, lifted his head, and looked into Djemo's completely disfigured face:

"Get up, you scum, and get out, everybody out," he shouted. Pulling Djemo up by the hair, Ziga raised him to his feet. Djemo could barely stand up, but he managed to take one step and then another, with Asaf and Kiki following.

"On all fours, I said—like dogs!" Ziga bellowed, like a dictator. He forced the three men to crawl up to a puddle by the entrance to the White House and then ordered them to wash in the filthy water. Their hands trembling, they washed the blood off their faces. "The boys have been eating strawberries and got themselves a little red," said Ziga, laughing like a madman before he chased them all back into the White House. Another prisoner, Slavko Ecimovic, a Croat, and one of the first to rebel against local Serb rule, was in the same room where they had just been tortured. At least, it *seemed* like him. He was kneeling, all curled up, by the radiator. When he lifted his head, where his face should have been was nothing but the bloody, spongy tissue under the skin that had just been ripped off. Instead of eyes, two hollow sockets were filled with black, coagulated blood.

"You'll all end up like this, you and your families," Ziga said, taking on the airs of a military commander. "We killed his father and mother. And his wife. We'll get his kids. And yours, too, we'll kill you all." And with a wide swing of his leg, he kicked Djemo right in the face again with his boot. Djemo felt pieces of dried blood flying out of his mouth and nose and shards of broken teeth cutting his tongue. Then everything stopped—the blows, the curses, even the screams seemed to subside. As if through a fog, Djemo saw someone in an officer's uniform enter the room. In response to some tacit command, the beating had stopped. The prisoners were taken out to be washed at the same puddle and then returned to the dorms. Slavko Ecimovic stayed in the White House and was never seen again.

Recovery

Djemo went first. When he opened the door to the dorm, the murmur of voices inside stopped. A hush came over the room. He held his arms out, barely able to see the people backing up in front of him to clear the way. And then a shrill scream: "Daddy!" Djemo felt his son's arms clutch him before he sank into the deepest abyss. His body was overcome by absolute dark and silence. He didn't know how much time had gone by before he heard indistinct voices and felt something cold on his face and body. He tried to open his eyes. He felt a sharp pain in his head. As wet and cold compresses were applied to his face and back, Djemo managed to notice, though only with great effort, the many people around him and the tearful face of his son.

His recovery lasted twenty days. During that time he couldn't even move. Ari and some other prisoners had to carry him to the toilet. It didn't make Djemo feel very good, having everyone else do things for him. He couldn't even get to the canteen to eat, so his mates would save up pieces of bread or an occasional biscuit, depriving themselves in order to give him something to eat. Every day Ari brought his father half of his own meal.

When Djemo looked at himself in the mirror for the first time, he started crying. His face was covered with black contusions and bruises. Where his nose had been, there was only a huge swelling that almost shut his eyes. Several of his front teeth were broken. His whole back was black and blue. The tracks of the endless blows converged into a single, dark surface that spread over his entire back and neck. Dr. Sadikovic told him later that his nose, a rib, and his right hand, at the wrist, were all broken, but that he would be all right: "You've pulled through. That's the most important thing. None of us thought you'd make it. At least now I can tell you, you're tough."

Chapter 3

The Siege of Sarajevo

Chapter Preface

Mourners who went to Lion Cemetery to bury their loved ones during the siege of Sarajevo had to worry about losing their own lives at the hands of Bosnian Serb snipers positioned in the hills surrounding the city. Lion Cemetery was safe compared with other burial places, however. A soccer field that had been converted into a cemetery was much more exposed to snipers, and the chances of being killed there were high. During the worst periods of shelling, residents in the besieged city had to bury their loved ones in the relative safety of their own backyards.

In Sarajevo, there were many ways to die. Bosnian Serbs bombed residences and public buildings. Simply walking down city streets was the most dangerous activity, for at any time, a Serb sniper or mortar shell might kill a pedestrian. With no running water and little food, Sarajevans also had to line up at springs and bakeries for scarce resources, which made them easy targets for gunmen.

In addition to those killed directly by mortar shells or bullets, many other civilians died as an indirect result of the war. For example, the siege cut off medical supplies such as antibiotics that were necessary to fight infection in those who had been hit by shrapnel and flying glass. Without the antibiotics, many of the wounded died. The lack of electricity made it difficult for people to heat their homes during the harsh Bosnian winters; as a result, many elderly residents living in convalescent homes died from the cold.

All told, more than ten thousand Sarajevans were killed during the siege. Those who survived try to deal with the loss of their loved ones who fell victim to the siege, and attempt to work through their anger at those who killed them. The treeless Lion Cemetery, with its rows of graves and plywood headstones, is a reminder of how tenuous the hopes of unity and reconciliation really are.

The Death of an Idea

Ed Vulliamy

> Bosnia's capital city of Sarajevo came under siege by the
> Bosnian Serbs in April 1992. Unable to leave the city or
> receive supplies from outside it, the residents of Sarajevo did
> their best to survive in increasingly difficult circumstances.
> Many outside observers wondered why more people had not
> attempted to flee the city before the siege or surrender to the
> Serbs at some point during the war.
>
> Journalist Ed Vulliamy, in the following excerpt from his
> book *Seasons in Hell*, explains that residents would not aban-
> don Sarajevo because to do so would be to surrender a dream.
> A cosmopolitan city where Serbs, Croats, and Muslims lived
> together harmoniously, Sarajevo was the testing ground for
> the idea that the Bosnian people could put historic hatreds
> aside and prosper as one people.

There is nothing quite like the Sarajevo feeling—the aura of a sophisticated capital city under siege, faced with the daily onslaught of an unseen army which enjoys an un- limited supply of armour and ammunition. In Sarajevo, you are never out of range. There is the Sarajevo walk: it is re- laxed only when protected by the cover of buildings or spe- cially constructed barricades; it becomes brisk and pur- poseful across a street, and breaks suddenly into a sprint over a patch of open ground, a cobbled forecourt or cross- roads exposed to the snipers' rifles, each with its own bloody history. As for the mortars and shells, they can drop anywhere, at any time, there is no protection. Not even at

From *Seasons in Hell: Understanding Bosnia's War*, by Ed Vulliamy. Copyright © 1994
by Ed Vulliamy. Reprinted by permission of St. Martin's Press, LLC.

night: one of the most extraordinary moments of all is when the sky above the city wrapped in darkness is suddenly illuminated by a flare sent up from the Serbian hilltops, which hangs there, diffusing its arrogant light; the wicked messenger. There is a short, ominous interval: the buildings of the city are dragged out of their hiding and displayed in a ghostly, menacing glow before the unseen gunners. Within thirty seconds, the shells hammer in. They may land a good few blocks away, the echo of their thud calling around the valleys, or they may land in the street below, the explosion sending people diving under tables, windows caving in across the room. Or they may land nearby, and thrust flying red-hot metal through the air, which can rip you to shreds.

Bedlam and Death

This is the sight and sound of Sarajevo: when the first shades of dusk have crept across the sky, people may be on the streets, huddled around the entrances to their flats or taking apart the remains of some rusty car that has been blasted off the road and abandoned; the lads are forever hungry for spare parts. Lovers (people do still fall in love in Sarajevo) sit in the porches, holding hands in solemn silence or talking in low voices and the old ladies may hurry home with a prized loaf of bread from the miraculously functioning bakery. Suddenly, two things happen within a split second but, curiously, in slow motion. There is a loud, angry whistling noise overhead, as though the air itself is being cut open and is letting out a cry of pain. It is a deep, not a shrill, whistle. It is a sound everyone knows, and as it proclaims itself we all duck, in perfect unison, torsos horizontal, necks craning to keep our heads raised so we do not bump into anything as we break into a run, and so we know whether we are still there or not. That moment freezes for what feels like a number of minutes, but which is no more than a nanosecond.

You can almost see the sound of the whistle through the air as the missile ploughs into the side of a block of flats: there is the crash of an explosion, a thud more than a bang, and a belch of black smoke. People do not scream like in the movies; apart from the explosion there seems to be very little other sound—for a moment. Then there is bedlam, rubble flung all over the road, breaking glass, a peculiar groan of tumbling bricks and masonry and the odd, blurted human exclamation. Then a scurrying in all directions, either to safety or, in the case of the brave, to find out the damage to the humans caught in the path of this latest pitiless bolt from the blue. On the occasion that the seventh shell in a week hit my friend Hasan's flats, the victim, apart from those caught by flying glass from an adjacent shop window, was a middle-aged woman—typical of Sarajevo's war. There was not as much blood as one might expect, apart from a thick, sticky stream that came from under her torn but still tied headscarf. Her clothes were ripped by the dozen or so pieces of shrapnel that had sprayed her body. The immediate reaction was to look into her eyes, open and only

The Destruction of Beauty

Residents of Sarajevo have always been extremely proud of their city. They claim that Sarajevo is the most cosmopolitan city in the Balkans where Serbs, Croats, Muslims and Jews live in the same apartment buildings and marry one another. However, when Bosnian Serbs lay siege to the city in the spring of 1992, Sarajevans witnessed the destruction of their city and its residents.

Kemal Kurspahic, editor-in-chief of the Oslobodjenje, *a daily Sarajevo newspaper, describes the damage that Serbian mortar shells have done to the city's most prized buildings. More important, he calculates the lives lost and bodies mutilated by Serb sniper fire, grenades, and shells, and wonders if Sarajevo will survive the war.*

Since the beginning of the Serbian aggression in April 1992, so much of Sarajevo's beauty has been destroyed. The hundred-year-old Austro-Hungarian city hall with its thousands of precious books and manuscripts; the main post office, also Austro-Hungarian; the picturesque Ottoman

recently functioning, and so it was a while before you noticed that her foot had been almost severed, still in its shoe and tied to her calves by tendons and sinews.

Her name was Amra Hadziskovic, and the most compelling thing about her death were the things of which her life had been apparently made on the last morning that she got up in her flat. You didn't have to pry to see what she had packed into the capacious burgundy leather handbag that was lying some six yards from her body: a pocket diary, a handkerchief, a list of some kind (unlikely to be a shopping list, they don't tend to make them in Sarajevo), a powder box, a cleanly sharpened pencil and some small plumbing fitting that maybe she had gone to try and replace in the ramshackle market. She had been a strong, finely built woman and had chosen a pair of sensible walking shoes and a long, brown, thick cotton skirt in which to do whatever

---

shops and the bazaars of Bascarsija; one of the most beautiful railway stations in Europe; the Winter Olympics sports halls, Zetra and Skenderija—all have been devastated by artillery fire. The same fate has been visited upon government and parliamentary offices and elegant commercial buildings, including the offices of my paper *Oslobodjenje*. The city's communication and transportation facilities are in ruins, as are its hospitals (targets of regular, systematic shelling), and more than half of its apartments have been destroyed. It is hard for a city to be the same as it was after such devastation.

But, above all, can Sarajevo survive the destruction of so many lives? More than ten thousand have been killed and a hundred thousand severely wounded. So many, too many, with arm or leg amputated, have been maimed and crippled for life. Tens of thousands have been separated from their families, not knowing what happened to their loved ones—captured, killed, driven out, made refugees—or whether they will ever see them again.

Kemae Kurspanic, "Is There a Future?" *Why Bosnia? Writings on the Balkan War,* ed. by Rabia Ali and Lawrence Lifschultz. Stony Creek, CT: Pamphleteer's Press, 1993.

Most war refugees were women, children, and the elderly. Many residents of Sarajevo remained in the city during the war.

business she had planned for that day. Now Amra had been killed by a shell that had come from what felt like nowhere. But that was an illusion. It had been loaded and fired by someone up there, and there would be tens of thousands more who would die like Amra.

Multicultural Crossroads

There is charisma as well as tragedy in the phenomenon of Sarajevo. The sight of such a city, trying to defend the eroding corners of bygone normal life, is something to behold. The Sarajevans have a certain dignity about them. They are generally courteous to each other; the girls—many of them very beautiful—take an almost absurd care over their appearance. Cosmetics rank with baby milk and cigarettes as the most prized commodities on the black market.

Sarajevo at the outset of the war was the symbol of a Bosnia that was the exact opposite to that of the War of Maps [which threatened to divide Bosnia along ethnic lines], and which its army and people were setting out to defend. It was a university city, which boasted one of the two great rock bands to come out of the old Yugoslavia, Bjelo

Dugme (White Button). It was a city made up of rogues in dirty suits, students with pony tails and earrings, old men with sticks and women in traditional headscarves, house-proud ladies and hospitality which can almost oppress a visitor. This was a crossroads between Europe and the Orient, where the *narod* dissolved. Sephardic Jews came here in flight from Spain, it was the 'Damascus of the North'; it was Muslim, Serb, Croatian, Austrian, Jewish and more besides. The maze of little lanes around the old Turkish Bascarsija market and the Ali Pasha mosque was teeming with cafés, flower stalls and the rough traders of trinketry, and the air was heavy with the smell *cevap* Turkish kebabs. But at each end of the lanes were the Orthodox church and the Catholic cathedral. Selection for the staging of the 1984 Winter Olympics made many Sarajevans feel that *their* Bosnia had been put on the map. My friend Bojan Zec returned just in time for the referendum [for Bosnia's independence] and the war, after eight months' study at Edinburgh University. Bojan is young and serious, now working for the government in an office whose windows are decked out with sandbags.

The Death of an Idea

'Sarajevo means more than appears to the outsider. The death of Sarajevo would be the death of an idea; if Sarajevo falls or is partitioned, then something dies psychologically as well as physically. We developed a way of life here through who our friends were and the kind of conversations we had. And suddenly we realise what that way of life was: we were going to shut out the historical hatreds. Quite unconsciously, this city was living what Bosnia is all about. But people are now conscious of this. Without it, we would be going mad, or would have opted for an easy life and surrendered. Under siege, the city has suddenly recognised itself.'

City of Terror

Elma Softić

> Everyday life in the besieged city of Sarajevo was filled with
> terror, death, and hardship. As the Bosnian Serbs tightened
> their hold on the city, most Sarajevans became increasingly
> desperate. In the following excerpts from her diary and per-
> sonal letters, Elma Softić describes her life in Sarajevo during
> the war. When the war began, Softić was a thirty-year-old
> philosophy teacher living with her middle-class family.
> Almost overnight, her life changed radically. In her writings
> she describes the gruesome deaths and mutilations that
> resulted from Serb bombings of the city and her emotional
> reactions to what she experienced. Softić survived the war
> and now works as a secretary for Marie Stopes International,
> a United Nations aid organization based in Bosnia.

*Editor's Note: The original editor and translator deleted portions
of Softić's diary and letters to omit repetitions or information of
a personal nature. Such deletions are indicated by a [. . .].*

13 April 1992

TV Belgrade [in Serbia] is talking rubbish, like this: in the
Old City [of Sarajevo] people are blowing up their own
property themselves in order to provide a cover for their per-
secution of the Serbs.

And in other cities in Bosnia-Herzegovina, chaos: Vise-
grad, Foca, Kupres, Bosanski Brod, Mostar, Capljina.

Refugees are streaming in all directions.

Reprinted with the permission of Key Porter Books from *Sarajevo Days, Sarajevo Nights*,
by Elma Softić. Copyright © Elma Softić, 1995.

21 April 1992

At 4:55 this morning the bombardment of Sarajevo began. There was shelling across the entire city, but mostly in the old part. The Electric Company building was bombarded, GRAS *[Gradski Autobusni Saobracaj = city transit]* once again. It went on till after 8 a.m.

All day long you could hear bursts of machine-gun fire, single shots, and distant explosions.

Around 5:30 p.m. the bombardment started up again. That was the worst afternoon and the worst night so far. From half past five, when it started, it didn't stop until after two in the morning. It was terrifying listening to the approach of the explosions—every bomb that fell was nearer than the last. That's unendurable—you're just waiting to be blown to pieces. You breathe a sigh of relief when you hear one fall farther away than the preceding one—it's receding. And it doesn't let up. There were several times when I was certain that the bomb had landed on the pavement in front of our building. It was horrific. The five of us squeezed into that corner by the main door—crammed into two square metres—and waited for it to pass.

When the first shell landed in our immediate vicinity, I got diarrhea. [My sister] Ilona is frightened. So is Dad. You can read Mom's terror and despair on her face. My terror manifests itself in irritability. I curse, I shout, everything annoys me.

Now, at 3:35 A.M., instead of sleeping (things have quieted down), I'm writing. I wish I could describe to you the terror and anxiety I felt. All I know is that I was afraid, that I had diarrhea, and that I was covered in a cold sweat. Shudders of horror went through me, my throat was constantly constricted, and I thought that I wouldn't be able to stand it, that I would simply die.

11 May 1992

God created this world. But not out of His goodness; no, it arose from the filthy scourings of the evil cleansed from His own soul. And He, newly pure, went far away from here.

27 May 1992

A massacre in Vaso Miskin Street, in front of Planika, where people were waiting for the bread truck. Three shells landed in the crowd. The bloody bread of Sarajevo. There were about 200 people there. A slaughterhouse. The street running with blood. People lying, mown down. A torn-off foot. Some people are moving, some are screaming for help, others are motionless. The uninjured are running. Some are trying to help—they're carrying away the wounded. You can see shattered legs. One woman's foot is hanging, barely attached, a man being carried by two others has legs that are hanging at a most unnatural angle. A heap of human meat. Blood, body bits. People are arriving in automobiles and trucks, rushing out from the neighbouring homes in their slippers, wringing their hands, weeping, running, looking for the living—the dead can wait.

At 1:35 P.M. they are reading out the names: 124 injured and 12 dead.

As of 8 p.m.—16 dead and 144 wounded.

The maternity hospital has burned down. Up to now, 171,000 children have been born in the hospital. Maybe it was the papa of one of them who set it on fire. Three babies died—from the effects of the bombardment. Because of the power outage the incubators stopped working.

Part of the Marshal Tito barracks is on fire, as are the School of Electrical Engineering and the School of Economics.

The last time I was in the school, I went round the classrooms—the windowpanes shattered, a huge hole in the wall on the third floor, and on one desk the graffito: "Death to fascism, and dammit, to the people, too."

Well, fascism is on the increase, but the people are dying.

6 July 1992

The twelve-year-old girl who was wounded in [the Sarajevo suburb of] Dobrinja, while she was sleeping in the same bed as her little cousin whose head was partly blown away by shrapnel, was the daughter of Vesna Sokcevic! Dreadful.

Dreadful. The children had come up from the shelter to relax and take a nap in a normal bed, since it looked as though the shelling had stopped. The little boy, Filip Simic, was killed (I remember the eyewitness news report from the man who had run into the room first, a neighbour who was in the apartment at the time and who said that on the pillow, instead of the child's head, was a bloody stain). Vesna's daughter sustained severe head injuries and her chances of recovery, at least given the present conditions and facilities here in Sarajevo, are exceedingly slim. The child needs to be sent abroad for medical treatment, and it looks as though they have got permission to do so from UNPROFOR [the United Nations Protection Force], or from whichever of those powerful world organizations that deals with such matters, and that they will be leaving soon.

Poor Vesna! Poor little girl! All parents and all children who have stayed in this ghastly city are to be pitied. I don't understand, I don't understand, I don't understand.

26 July 1992

There's nothing I can do to rid myself of the grief that has been choking me since yesterday. I cannot comprehend, I cannot accept that Yasmin *[the son of Elma's aunt Raja]* is dead. He's gone. He's buried under two metres of earth. He was life itself, fullness, abundance, joy.

But one day, even to his own parents, he will seem like a dream.

Seven and a half thousand children in Bosnia-Herzegovina will, according to current estimates, remain permanent invalids. Seven and a half thousand in four and a half months! This land has endured all manner of horrors through its history, but never before now has it been trodden by more lame than hale people, yet it appears that this time is approaching. Already I am encountering the maimed in the street: in wheelchairs—with both legs missing; on crutches—with legs cut off below the ankle or knee or hip. Missing arms, or several fingers or whole hands, with scars, their stumps wrapped in white bandages, empty sleeves and empty trouser legs. It scares me—it seems to me that when it's all over, this will be an accursed city of cripples who will drift like ghosts amid the ruins. And their single purpose will be just this: to drift amid the ruins.

29 December 1992

People are dying of cold and hunger.

The parks of Sarajevo have been laid waste—in the park around the Austrian house not a single tree is standing. The birches along the colonnade that leads to the cable railway no longer exist. The trees lining one side of the boulevard from the market near the National Library to the Hotel National— some 350 metres—are missing. In the park by the kindergarten in the same street—not a single tree, just the day-care building, totally devastated, but not by a mortar shell. People have stripped the roofing and all the wood from the structure: even termites could not have done a better job. People are walking around the city carrying axes and saws. They chop down the massive old shade trees, but also the young saplings, no thicker than your hand. The saddest sight of all is the people who show up late, after some tree has been "executed," and gather the splinters, the sawdust, the twigs, and the bark that have been left behind. They wander around through the devastated parks, with straw bags, plastic bags, baskets, and numb with cold, scoop up the debris.

Desperate people are sifting through trash heaps looking for heating fuel [. . .] (they say that old Adidas and plastic slippers burn the best). To say nothing of the fact that basements are being cleared of old furniture—by those who have some; those who do not are starting to burn woodwork and furniture that is still in use.

16 December 1993

[a continuation of her letter to (her friend) Caka]
Fuck, the minute I even think that in some book of world history some asshole is going to write about this war as a conflict of national and religious interests between ethnic groups located in the perpetually unstable region of the Balkans,

which lasted from 1991 to whenever, I could just blow this whole planet to bits so that not a particle of it remains.

Meanwhile, here there is terror, blood, and death. [. . .] There isn't a square inch of pavement in Sarajevo that hasn't had blood spilled on it. Can you believe it—the rain came down all that afternoon, the whole night and the next morning, and it still didn't wash away the blood of the unfortunates who died *hungry,* for in this town everyone is hungry, *dirty,* for in this town water is measured out in coffee spoons, and *terrified,* for there isn't a person on these streets whose sweat doesn't smell of fear. Puddles of blood have collected in the holes made by shrapnel and in the dust from the façades and bricks turned to powder by the bombs. It's not the first time I've walked through human blood—that's a normal thing in Sarajevo—but I can't fathom how much blood there must have been for it not to have been washed away by the rain.

A Child's View of War

Zlata Filipovic

During the Bosnian war, thousands of children became trapped in Sarajevo with their families when Bosnian Serbs lay siege to the city in April of 1992. Zlata Filipovic, an eleven-year-old girl living in Sarajevo with her family when the war began, kept a diary of her experiences during the siege. In her diary, which she addresses as "Mimmy," Zlata recounts her family's efforts to survive and describes the destruction of Sarajevo. Zlata's diary reveals her transformation from a happy schoolgirl to an angry, frightened survivor. Zlata submitted her diary in 1993 to her teacher, who then had it published with the help of UNICEF. Zlata survived the war and now lives in Paris, France.

Friday, April 3, 1992

Dear Mimmy,

Mommy is at work. Daddy has gone to Zenica. I'm home from school and have been thinking. Azra leaves for Austria today. She's afraid of war. HEY! Still, I keep thinking about what Aunt Melica heard at the hairdresser's. What do I do if they bomb Sarajevo? Safia is here, and I'm listening to Radio-M. I feel safer.

Mommy says that what Melica heard at the hairdresser's is misinformation. I hope so!

Daddy came back from Zenica all upset. He says there are terrible crowds at the train and bus stations. People are

From *Zlata's Diary,* by Zlata Filipovic. Copyright © 1994 by Editions Robert Laffont/ Fixot. Reprinted with permission from Viking Penguin, a division of Penguin Putnam, Inc.

leaving Sarajevo. Sad scenes. They're the people who believe the misinformation [that a war is eminent]. Mothers
and children are leaving, the fathers are staying behind, or
just children are leaving, while their parents stay. Everybody
is in tears.

Daddy says he wishes he hadn't seen that.
Love you, Mimmy,
Zlata

Sunday, April 12, 1992

Dear Mimmy,

The new sections of town—Dobrinja, Mojmilo, Vojnicko
polje—are being badly shelled. Everything is being destroyed, burned, the people are in shelters. Here in the middle of town, where we live, it's different. It's quiet. People
go out. It was a nice warm spring day today. We went out
too. Vaso Miskin Street was full of people, children. It looked
like a peace march. People came out to be together, they
don't want war. They want to live and enjoy themselves the
way they used to. That's only natural, isn't it? Who likes or
wants war, when it's the worst thing in the world?

I keep thinking about the march I joined today. It's bigger
and stronger than war. That's why it will win. The people
must be the ones to win, not the war, because war has nothing to do with humanity. War is something inhuman.
Zlata

Saturday, April 18, 1992

Dear Mimmy,

There's shooting, shells are falling. This really is WAR.
Mommy and Daddy are worried, they sit up until late at
night, talking. They're wondering what to do, but it's hard
to know. Whether to leave and split up, or stay here together.
Keka wants to take me to Ohrid. Mommy can't make up her
mind—she's constantly in tears. She tries to hide it from me,
but I see everything. I see that things aren't good here.
There's no peace. War has suddenly entered our town, our
homes, our thoughts, our lives. It's terrible.

It's also terrible that Mommy has packed my suitcase.
Love,
Zlata

Saturday, May 2, 1992

Dear Mimmy,

Today was truly, absolutely the worst day ever in Sarajevo. The shooting started around noon. Mommy and I moved into the hall. Daddy was in his office, under our apartment, at the time. We told him on the intercom to run quickly to the downstairs lobby where we'd meet him. We brought Cicko [Zlata's canary] with us. The gunfire was getting worse, and we couldn't get over the wall to the Bobars', so we ran down to our own cellar.

The cellar is ugly, dark, smelly. Mommy, who's terrified of mice, had two fears to cope with. The three of us were in the same corner as the other day. We listened to the pounding shells, the shooting, the thundering noise overhead. We even heard planes. At one moment I realized that this awful cellar was the only place that could save our lives. Suddenly, it started to look almost warm and nice. It was the only way we could defend ourselves against all this terrible shooting. We heard glass shattering in our street. Horrible. I put my fingers in my ears to block out the terrible sounds. I was worried about Cicko. We had left him behind in the lobby. Would he catch cold there? Would something hit him? I was terribly hungry and thirsty. We had left our half-cooked lunch in the kitchen.

When the shooting died down a bit, Daddy ran over to our apartment and brought us back some sandwiches. He said he could smell something burning and that the phones weren't working. He brought our TV set down to the cellar. That's when we learned that the main post office (near us) was on fire and that they had kidnapped [Bosnian] President [Izetbegovic]. At around 8:00 we went back up to our apartment. Almost every window in our street was broken. Ours were all right, thank God. I saw the post office in flames. A terrible sight. The fire-fighters battled with the raging fire.

Daddy took a few photos of the post office being devoured by the flames. He said they wouldn't come out because I had been fiddling with something on the camera. I was sorry. The whole apartment smelled of the burning fire. God, and I used to pass by there every day. It had just been done up. It was huge and beautiful, and now it was being swallowed up by the flames. It was disappearing. That's what this neighborhood of mine looks like, my Mimmy. I wonder what it's like in other parts of town? I heard on the radio that it was awful around the Eternal Flame. The place is knee-deep in glass. We're worried about Grandma and Granddad. They live there. Tomorrow, if we can go out, we'll see how they are. A terrible day.

This has been the worst, most awful day in my eleven-year-old life. I hope it will be the only one. Mommy and Daddy are very edgy. I have to go to bed.

Ciao!
Zlata

Wednesday, May 27, 1992

Dear Mimmy,

SLAUGHTER! MASSACRE! HORROR! CRIME! BLOOD! SCREAMS! TEARS! DESPAIR!

That's what Vaso Miskin Street looks like today. Two shells exploded in the street and one in the market. Mommy was nearby at the time. She ran to Grandma and Granddad's. Daddy and I were beside ourselves because she hadn't come home. I saw some of it on TV but I still can't believe what I actually saw. It's unbelievable. I've got a lump in my throat and a knot in my tummy. HORRIBLE. They're taking the wounded to the hospital. It's a madhouse. We kept going to the window hoping to see Mommy, but she wasn't back. They released a list of the dead and wounded. Daddy and I were tearing our hair out. We didn't know what had happened to her. Was she alive? At 4:00, Daddy decided to go and check the hospital. He got dressed, and I got ready to go to the Bobars', so as not to stay at home alone. I looked out the window one more time and . . . I SAW

MOMMY RUNNING ACROSS THE BRIDGE. As she came into the house she started shaking and crying. Through her tears she told us how she had seen dismembered bodies. All the neighbors came because they had been afraid for her. Thank God, Mommy is with us. Thank God. A HORRIBLE DAY. UNFORGETTABLE. HORRIBLE! HORRIBLE!

Your Zlata

Monday, June 29, 1992

Dear Mimmy,

BOREDOM!!! SHOOTING!!! SHELLING!!! PEOPLE BEING KILLED!!! DESPAIR!!! HUNGER!!! MISERY!!! FEAR!!!

That's my life! The life of an innocent eleven-year-old schoolgirl!! A schoolgirl without a school, without the fun and excitement of school. A child without games, without friends, without the sun, without birds, without nature, without fruit, without chocolate or sweets, with just a little powdered milk. In short, a child without a childhood. A wartime child. I now realize that I am really living through a war, I am witnessing an ugly, disgusting war. I and thousands of other children in this town that is being destroyed, that is crying, weeping, seeking help, but getting none. God, will this ever stop, will I ever be a schoolgirl again, will I ever enjoy my childhood again? I once heard that childhood is the most wonderful time of your life. And it is. I loved it, and now an ugly war is taking it all away from me. Why? I feel sad. I feel like crying. I am crying.

Your Zlata

Thursday, November 19, 1992

Dear Mimmy,

Nothing new on the political front. They are adopting some resolutions, the "kids [politicians]" are negotiating, and we are dying, freezing, starving, crying, parting with our friends, leaving our loved ones.

I keep wanting to explain these stupid politics to myself,

because it seems to me that politics caused this war, making it our everyday reality. War has crossed out the day and replaced it with horror, and now horrors are unfolding instead of days. It looks to me as though these politics mean Serbs, Croats and Muslims. But they are all people. They are all the same. They all look like people, there's no difference. They all have arms, legs and heads, they walk and talk, but now there's "something" that wants to make them different.

Among my girlfriends, among our friends, in our family, there are Serbs and Croats and Muslims. It's a mixed group and I never knew who was a Serb, a Croat or a Muslim. Now politics has started meddling around. It has put an "S" on Serbs, an "M" on Muslims and a "C" on Croats, it wants to separate them. And to do so it has chosen the worst, blackest pencil of all—the pencil of war which spells only misery and death.

Why is politics making us unhappy, separating us, when we ourselves know who is good and who isn't? We mix with the good, not with the bad. And among the good there are Serbs and Croats and Muslims, just as there are among the bad. I simply don't understand it. Of course, I'm "young," and politics are conducted by "grown-ups." But I think we "young" would do it better. We certainly wouldn't have chosen war.

The "kids" really are playing, which is why us kids are not playing, we are living in fear, we are suffering, we are not enjoying the sun and flowers, we are not enjoying our childhood. WE ARE CRYING.

A bit of philosophizing on my part, but I was alone and felt I could write this to you, Mimmy. You understand me. Fortunately, I've got you to talk to.

And now,

Love,

Zlata

Monday, March 15, 1993

Dear Mimmy,

I'm sick again. My throat hurts, I'm sneezing and coughing. And spring is around the corner. The second spring of the war. I know from the calendar, but I don't see it. I can't see it because I can't feel it. All I can see are the poor people still lugging water, and the even poorer invalids—young people without arms and legs. They're the ones who had the fortune or perhaps the misfortune to survive.

There are no trees to blossom and no birds, because the war has destroyed them as well. There is no sound of birds twittering in springtime. There aren't even any pigeons—the symbol of Sarajevo. No noisy children, no games. Even the children no longer seem like children. They've had their childhood taken away from them, and without that they can't be children. It's as if Sarajevo is slowly dying, disappearing. Life is disappearing. So how can I feel spring, when spring is something that awakens life, and here there is no life, here everything seems to have died.

I'm sad again, Mimmy. But you have to know that I'm getting sadder and sadder. I'm sad whenever I think, and I have to think.

Your Zlata

Saturday, August 21, 1993

Dear Mimmy,

Everybody is in a bad mood these days. Mommy, Daddy, my Uncle Braco, Aunt Melica, Grandma, Granddad . . . I don't know, everybody's quite edgy.

Did I tell you, Mimmy, that Kenan (Melica's son) is in the hospital? Wait, wait, no, he's not wounded. There's no injury. He's sick. He has jaundice. From the water, probably, because they get their water from a spring and it looks as if that spring isn't "pure." And there seems to be an epidemic in that part of town.

My best friend Mirna was here yesterday. Even she isn't quite right.

The day before yesterday I was at my cousin Diana's. We watched two movies: *Purple Rain* and *Breakfast at Tiffany's*. Audrey Hepburn is really cute. Do you know she died? Yes, she died about two months ago, maybe more.

Yesterday I got an A in my piano exam. Super.

The political situation? A STUPID MESS. Maybe that's why everybody is so edgy. The "kids" are trying to come to some agreement again. They're drawing maps, coloring with their crayons, but I think they're crossing out human beings, childhood and everything that's nice and normal. They really are just like kids.

There's no mail. I don't know why, but nobody has been getting any mail lately.

Zlata

Friday, September 17, 1993

Dear Mimmy,

The "kids" are negotiating something, signing something. Again giving us hope that this madness will end. There's supposed to be a cease-fire tomorrow and on September 21 at Sarajevo airport everybody is supposed to sign FOR PEACE. Will the war stop on the day that marks the change from one season to another???

With all the disappointments I've had with previous truces and signatures, I can't believe it.

I can't believe it because another horrible shell fell today, ending the life of a three-year-old little boy, wounding his sister and mother.

All I know is that the result of their little games is 15,000 dead in Sarajevo, 3,000 of them children, 50,000 permanent invalids, whom I already see in the streets on crutches, in wheelchairs, armless and legless. And I know that there's no room left in the cemeteries and parks to bury the latest victims.

Maybe that's why this madness should stop.

Your Zlata

Sunday, October 17, 1993

Dear Mimmy,

Yesterday our friends [the Bosnian Serbs] in the hills reminded us of their presence and that they are now in control and can kill, wound, destroy . . . yesterday was a truly horrible day.

Five hundred and ninety shells. From 4:30 in the morning on, throughout the day. Six dead and fifty-six wounded. That is yesterday's toll. Souk-bunar fared the worst. I don't know how Melica is. They say that half the houses up there are gone.

We went down into the cellar. Into the cold, dark, stupid cellar which I hate. We were there for hours and hours. They kept pounding away. All the neighbors were with us.

AGAIN! Again and again they keep sinking all our boats, taking and burning all our hopes. People said that they wouldn't do it anymore. That there would soon be an end to it, that everything would resolve itself. THAT THIS STUPID WAR WOULD END!

Oh God, why do they spoil everything? Sometimes I think it would be better if they kept shooting, so that we wouldn't find it so hard when it starts up again. This way, just as you relax, it starts up AGAIN. I am convinced now that it will never end.

Because some people don't want it to, some evil people who hate children and ordinary folk.

I keep thinking that we're alone in this hell, that nobody is thinking of us, nobody is offering us a helping hand. But there are people who are thinking and worrying about us.

Yesterday the Canadian TV crew and [British journalist] Janine [Di Giovanni] came to see how we had survived the mad shelling. That was nice of them. Really kind.

And when we saw that Janine was holding an armful of food, we got so sad we cried. Alexandra came too.

People worry about us, they think about us, but sub-humans want to destroy us. Why? I keep asking myself why?

We haven't done anything. We're innocent. But helpless!
Zlata

Sarajevo Wounded

Ellen Blackman

As a result of daily sniper fire and mortar shells exploding on the city, Sarajevo's hospitals were inundated with wounded. Without electricity and water, hospital staff could only perform the most routine operations. In addition, within the first months of the war, medical supplies such as antibiotics and painkillers ran out. To make matters worse, the Bosnian Serb Army frequently targeted the hospital in an effort to impede efforts to save the wounded, which imperiled the lives of the doctors and nurses who worked there.

During a mission to save Sarajevan children who had been wounded in the war, American writer and photographer Ellen Blackman visited the Sarajevo State Hospital. In the following excerpt from her book, *Harvest in the Snow*, Blackman describes the condition of the hospital, the wounded that were recovering there, and the determined staff who worked around the clock to help them. She recounts how she was ultimately successful in getting one critically injured girl airlifted out of Sarajevo where the child could receive proper medical attention.

A s we walked, I pointed to the remains of what appeared to have been a large yellow building. [My Bosnian friend] Almir identified what was left of it as the old surgery unit of the state hospital. He said the Serbs had burned it down early on. As unconscionable as it was, the Serbs had made the hospitals their first targets. I could see the tension here; it was on all the faces of all the people in the crowd— the children, the young people, the elderly, everyone. Even

From *Harvest in the Snow: My Crusade to Rescue the Lost Children of Bosnia,* by Ellen Blackman. Copyright © 1997 by Brassey's. Reprinted with permission from Brassey's.

the mongrels moved along at a fast pace. A pedestrian on this street had to be alert to what was going around him at all times. He had to have a quick step; daydreaming could prove fatal. Almir said, "This is a war waged against civilians, and children are no exception. The youngsters in Sarajevo have become little experts on munitions. They have learned to distinguish the various types of Serbian weaponry. Even the smallest among them will tell you what the hissing noise of a Serb mortar shell sounds like and how many millimeters it is. They have learned to know whether Serb antiaircraft fire is just out of range or whether it is time for them to interrupt their play and run." . . .

We were just at the foot of the front drive of the hospital when the shelling grew louder. Some of the pedestrians crouched low and began to run, a sign that the snipers were targeting dangerously close. A young Bosnian policeman standing guard by the front of the hospital warned us to move indoors. We quickly made our way up the drive and into the hospital's only functional entrance, the emergency room.

Sarajevo State Hospital

After chasing ghosts for so long, I had finally come face-to-face with the Sarajevo State Hospital. All those horrible films of it back home that had prompted me to come to Sarajevo had become reality, and nothing about my perception had been exaggerated. It was the same grim and desperate plea that I had envisioned it to be. Its inner corridor was stifling hot; and its dim lighting, derived solely from natural sources of daylight because of the absence of electricity, threw a grayish hue over the place. The hospital halls were lined with old run-down gurneys, and from their haphazard positions it appeared that their last use had been harried and frantic. Several of them even had a considerable amount of fresh blood on them. I watched as an orderly on his hands and knees tried to wash up some of the blood that had splattered onto the floor below.

A young, pale, obviously pregnant nurse came out and greeted us. I couldn't begin to imagine what it must have been like to carry a child in such uncertain times. Since she didn't speak English, Almir had to translate. He told her we were there to see Dr. Karaikovic, and she nodded for us to follow her. She led us past the ER and into a small private waiting area where she signaled for us to take a seat. Several people were sleeping on cots scattered around the room, and there was a man sitting behind a battered desk and pecking away at an ancient typewriter. The windows behind him were broken and patched over with wooden slats just like the windows in the ER room. All the walls showed bullet holes, and from the great numbers of them and their wide range of dispersal, it was obvious that the hospital was no safe place to be.

Double Shifts

As soon as we were settled into some chairs, the young nurse rushed off to alert Dr. Karaikovic. The man seated at the typewriter looked up and in fairly good English introduced himself as Dr. Mirza Begovic. "Please excuse the people on the cots," he apologized. "We have been working double shifts. I have just gotten off a forty-five-hour duty. Most of us haven't seen our own beds in days." Then, right on cue, the keen Sarajevan sense of humor surfaced. "None of us here worry, though, that our spouses will leave us in our absence. You see, the lack of transportation here has lowered our divorce rate considerably." He went on to say, "I cannot guarantee when Dr. Karaikovic will be down. He may be some time since we are having a busy morning here. Many sniper victims were brought in early this morning, and the doctors are up there doing amputations. Everything is so backed up. We have only one surgery gallery open today. Just to do a surgery each doctor must drag all his equipment along, and we must share the same tiny portable generator." I asked the doctor why they didn't use a larger generator. "It just isn't practical," he said. "We haven't the fuel with which to run it. In fact, we haven't been able to do anything here other than emergency surgeries for weeks now."

"How do you manage to run the ventilators and the respirators for all your critical care patients?" I asked. His answer was startling.

"By hand," he replied, "in shifts." I was just beginning to get an idea of some of the hidden ramifications that the Serbian fuel embargo had on Sarajevo. He went on to reveal the scope of the problem. "This lack of fuel has been quite devastating to everyone. It touches us all in one way or another. For example, we are in a real crisis with our diabetics. With no working refrigerators, our insulin has all gone bad. There is just no way to keep it. Do you know right now we haven't one drop of insulin in Sarajevo? We haven't had any for months. The pediatric units are crammed full of juvenile diabetics. Many of them are dying needlessly. The letter that I am now preparing is for a physician colleague of mine in Germany. As futile as it may seem, I am asking him if he can provide us with some kind of help.

After a short while, the pregnant nurse reappeared with some hot coffee. Dr. Begovic told me she had to prepare it on an open fire. I watched as she served it. Although she looked fatigued, she worked with great efficiency. I began to appreciate the energy and selfless effort the staff at Sarajevo State was putting out; even the smallest of tasks was difficult.

A Horror Show

It was more than an hour before Dr. Karaikovic finally made an appearance. He took Almir and me up to the orthopedic clinic, where I passed Eddie's picture around among the staff.[1] One of the nurses said she thought she recognized him, but she said it had been months since she had seen him there. She tried to look up his name in the clinic records but found no known address listed for him. She said she didn't know how I could locate him. Dr. Karaikovic explained, "We are so flooded with patients like Eddie that it becomes impossible to keep up with all of them. Fresh cases come pouring in here nearly every day. There are scores of young people like him all over Sarajevo." I had been dealt a tough blow.

---

1. Eddie was a sick child whom the author was trying to get out of the country in order to get him medical help.

Dr. Karaikovic suggested I have a look around for him anyway, just to be sure. He had been right. As I went from ward to ward, I saw many young people. Most of them were military-age young men, ranging anywhere from around Eddie's age [in their early teens] to their early twenties. It was like a horror show. Many of them were missing limbs, some had lost both their arms, and others had lost their legs. Many had badly scarred faces from land mines and exploding mortar shells. As I searched for Eddie's face among them, they stared out at me through hollow eyes. Once strapping, handsome young men, they were now reduced to the shallow image of frail ghosts wasting away. I had to turn away.

The whole depressing experience had left me feeling ashamed as a human being that none of us were doing anything to stop the atrocity. It all seemed so hopeless. I said good-bye to Dr. Karaikovic . . . . When we reached the end of the long, dark corridor of the orthopedic clinic, one of the doctors came running after us. She told us that if we really wanted to help someone, there was a child in desperate need. She said we should go up to the intensive-care surgery unit and ask for Dr. Edo Jaganjac. Almir and I clung tightly to the banister as we made out way up the pitch-black stairwell to the fourth floor.

Whimpering in Pain

We found the child whimpering in pain. She was only five years old, and her name was Irma Hadzimuratovic. Curled up in a fetal position and sucking her thumb, she had a thick wad of bandages wrapped around her small abdomen. Her father sat numbly on a chair near her bedside with his face buried in his hands. Irma had silky, freshly bobbed brown hair and a tiny pug nose. Her small fingernails still bore a splash of the pink polish her mom had put there the week before.

Her physician, Dr. Edo Jaganjac, hovered over the bed looking anxious and exhausted. He had black circles under his eyes. He told me the child had been critically injured by a mortar shell; her mother had been killed by the same shell. Mercifully, Irma's little sister had survived the attack because of the selfless act of a neighbor who had shielded the little girl's body with her own. She, too, lay injured in another hospital, her exact whereabouts and condition unknown. The mortar attack had left Irma with some serious abdominal and spinal injuries. In addition, the child was burning up with fever from infection. Dr. Jaganjac had already performed several emergency surgeries to stabilize her, and had removed much of her intestine. He told us she needed more surgery at a better-equipped hospital. He explained, "I've done all that I can for her. It's impossible to do anything more. She needs complicated surgery, and we're just not equipped for it. We haven't even the basics here. There aren't any painkillers or antibiotics for her, not even simple aspirin. She has been suffering for more than seven days now." He told me it was agonizing for the entire staff to watch her slowly deteriorate. I asked him why she hadn't been airlifted out to another hospital. Dr. Jaganjac replied, I've been pleading with the UN for days now to take her out. Sometimes I send up to three messages a day. I was told the UN doctor assigned here was in Zagreb [Croatia]. They told me nothing could be done until he gave the word to sign her out. They repeatedly tell me he is aware of her condition, yet he leaves no orders for her to go."

Every so often, Irma would open her sky-blue eyes wide and look up at us. She was such a little fighter who was suffering so badly without her mother to comfort her. I could see no possible excuse or reasonable answer why this child was being ignored by the UN. I asked the doctor if she still had a chance. Dr. Jaganjac replied, "Yes, but only if she gets proper care in a fully equipped hospital outside Sarajevo." He added, "She doesn't have much time left. She needs to go within the next day or two at most." Then he pointed to the way Irma's body was positioning itself. He said she was developing complications; her curved posturing was a sign of brain damage setting in. I told the doctor that I would be back to make a film about Irma to pressure the UN into taking her out. I asked Almir if he would help, and he told me to count him in.

Chapter 4

The Media

Chapter Preface

Women journalists—"chicks in the zone," as some female journalists called themselves—were responsible for publicizing the systematic rapes that occurred in the Bosnian war. According to the Bosnian government commission on war crimes in Sarajevo, thirty thousand Muslim and Croat women were raped by Serbs in the first year of the war. The Ministry for Interior Affairs places the figure at fifty thousand. Through extensive and ongoing interviews with rape victims, women journalists were able to tell the world about the brutal sex crimes committed by Bosnian Serbs. Largely as a result of these journalists' efforts, for the first time in history the International Criminal Tribunals court—which tries war crimes—defined rape as a crime against humanity.

Maggie O'Kane, a journalist for the *Guardian,* estimates that 40 percent of the journalists covering the war were women, many more than have covered past wars. She acknowledges that male journalists such as Roy Gutman from *Newsday* did an excellent job of covering the rapes but speculates that female journalists, because they were women and could empathize with the victims, were more insistent on publicizing the abuse of women. New York filmmaker Mandy Jacobson suggests that the rapes in Bosnia forced female journalists to consider the plight of women worldwide. Jadranka Cigelj—a rape victim whom Jacobson interviewed for her film *Calling the Ghosts: A Story About Rape, War, and Women*—says that maybe what happened to her is "God's revenge for her not noticing the suffering of other women in the past." Jacobson argues that, without journalists, the rapes would not have been exposed and eventually stopped.

The important role that journalists have played in Bosnia continues. The International Criminal Tribunals for the

Former Yugoslavia has called on many journalists to be expert witnesses against Serbian war criminals. As a result, the world community now recognizes rape as a crime against humanity. "Chicks in the zone" broadcast to the world how extensively rape is used as a tactic of war to humiliate victims, to entertain enemy soldiers, and to impregnate victims with the enemy's children. The coverage of rape by female journalists shamed politicians back home and led to efforts to close the rape camps, assist the victims, and punish those who committed these crimes.

The Media Saved Sarajevo

David Rieff

During the Bosnian war, many international journalists traveled to the country in order to cover the action. On the ground in the war zone, journalists were able to talk to people on all sides of the conflict and make their own assessments of the war. News reports from the region began to sympathize with the Bosnian government and depict the Bosnian Serbs as the aggressors. The United Nations, an international organization charged with keeping the peace in Bosnia, tried to remain impartial and accused journalists of hampering the peace effort by writing distorted accounts about the war.

In the following excerpt from his book *Slaughterhouse*, American journalist David Rieff defends the international media's coverage of the Bosnian war. Rieff, who lived off and on in Bosnia between 1992 and 1994, claims that he and other journalists witnessed too many Serb atrocities not to draw the conclusion that the Bosnian Serbs were guilty of committing genocide. He argues that the United Nations' generosity toward the Serbs made about as much sense as sympathizing with Hitler during World War II.

In the Lion Cemetery in Sarajevo in April 1993, an old man asked me, "Why do the Americans not drop the atom bomb on the Serbs?" A moment later, a mortar bomb exploded about three hundred meters away. The mourners—they had come to bury a fourteen-year-old boy killed by a

Reprinted with the permission of Simon & Schuster from *Slaughterhouse: Bosnia and the Failure of the West*, by David Rieff. Copyright © 1995 by David Rieff.

sniper two days before—ducked or, rather, went through a kind of pantomime of ducking for cover, since apart from the now shell-scarred statue of the lion and the plinth on which it stands in the center of the cemetery, there was no cover to speak of. Even the headstones in Sarajevo were being made of plywood after a year of the siege. And the gravediggers would tell you that the markers were of half the thickness they had been six months earlier. I stared edgily at two freshly dug graves ten meters down one of the burial rows. From past experience I knew they would be the safest places to crouch if the shelling began in earnest. That was always a distinct possibility since the Serb forces in the hills surrounding the city had made something of a specialty of firing on mourners as they buried their dead.

Carthage in Slow Motion

By Sarajevo standards, the Lion Cemetery was safer than the other main local graveyards. It was not nearly so exposed as the soccer pitch nearby, which had been converted into a cemetery by the local authorities in the fall of 1992 to take the overflow from the Kosevo Hospital morgue, and a year later was more than a third filled with graves. Until the cease-fire in February 1994, every part of Sarajevo was dangerous, and almost no place out of reach either of mortar or artillery fire, or of the ubiquitous snipers. At least shelling is relatively impersonal. Gunners aim at a neighborhood or, often, at a particular building. But what is especially frightening and degrading about being under sniper fire is that the sniper is picking and choosing from among the people who pass through the cross hairs of his gunsights. He is saying to himself, "I think I will shoot the girl in the red parka." Or he is saying, "I think I will let the tall man cross the road, but try to bring down his friend, the short unshaven guy in the wool coat, when he tries to follow."

That morning, before we set out for the Lion Cemetery, a French friend, a combat photographer of long experience, said to me, "There are two ways of photographing funerals: on your feet with the living, or on your knees with the dead." He might as well have been talking about the ways of thinking about Sarajevo, or generally about the slaughter in Bosnia. When one was in the city during the siege, what was overwhelming (apart from the fact that one was regularly frightened half out of one's wits) was that the situation seemed so simple. A European city was being reduced to nothing; Carthage [an ancient city in Africa that was defeated by the Romans in the second century B.C.E.] in slow motion, but this time with an audience and a videotaped record. Nothing, not the complex history of the region, nor the errors and crimes of the Bosnians themselves, nor the sometimes justified fears of the Bosnian Serbs, can mitigate the crime that took place. Nothing. Nothing. Nothing.

The CNN Effect

It was the conceit of journalists—made up, no doubt, partly of corporate self-regard, partly of an unexamined belief in progress and the pacifying effects of prosperity, and partly out of the self-congratulatory belief that Europe had become a civilized place—that if people back home could only be told and shown what was actually happening in Sarajevo, if they had to see on their television screens images of what a child who has just been hit by a soft-nosed bullet or a jagged splinter of shrapnel really looks like, or the bodies of citizens massacred as they queued for bread or water, then they would want their governments to do something. The hope of the Western press was that an informed citizenry back home would demand that their governments not allow the Bosnian Muslims to go on being massacred, raped, or forced from their homes. Instead, the sound bites and "visual bites" culled from the fighting bred casuistry and indifference far more regularly than it succeeded in mobilizing people to act or even to be indignant.

In retrospect, those of us who believed the result could have been otherwise were naive. There was a "CNN effect," in the broad sense that without CNN, the BBC [British Broadcasting Corporation], and the others showing it all the time, the Bosnian tragedy would have faded from people's minds after the first few months of fighting, even though it was taking place a couple of hundred miles from Italy. And, in a narrower sense, it really was the television cameras and not the North Atlantic Treaty Organization (NATO), let alone the United Nations (UN), that saved Sarajevo after the massacre in the Central Market in early February 1994. The British and the French, as well as the United Nations Protection Force (UNPROFOR) and the Department of Peacekeeping Operations, had resisted tooth and nail any credible threat on the part of the West to use force to defend Sarajevo for the better part of two years. They had insisted that the mandate did not permit it, that the risk to the humanitarian effort was too great, that in the end military threats would be counterproductive. But in the wake of the market massacre, they realized that there was real anger back home, for once, anger that would not be dissipated as easily as it had been in the wake of past atrocities. Unsurprisingly, they came to the conclusion that a number of steps previously deemed to have been impossible actually turned out to be quite doable after all. As a diplomat from one of the so-called Permanent Five countries on the [UN] Security Council [including the United States, China, France, the Russian Federation, and the United Kingdom] put it to me sardonically, "It is not the mandate but mass sentiments that have changed, particularly in Western Europe."

United Nations Impartiality

All along, it had been the task many of the journalists set themselves, consciously or unconsciously, to change the sentiments of their readers and viewers about the slaughter. That was why, throughout most of the siege, the reporters and television crews were perhaps the only dependable allies the Bosnians had. The Bosnian government, which had bet everything on foreign intervention, understood the influence of the press corps early on. It also understood that since it had been deprived by the continuation of the arms embargo of any means of defending itself effectively, eliciting foreign sympathy and raising money from the Islamic world were the only strong levers left at its disposal. But it was not true, as the United Nations people sometimes liked to suggest, that their sympathies caused the journalists to distort their stories to show the Bosnian government side in an undeservedly positive light. Indeed, the accusation testified more to the skewed morality that the commitment to impartiality in considering what they often called "the claims of the warring factions" had created among senior UN officials. For all their air of injured surprise, these officials must have known that if the Bosnian Serbs had any justice on their side, it came in about the same proportion as the Nazis' had, or the Khmer Rouge's [during the massacre in Cambodia]. Again, what the Serbs were doing was *genocide.*

What was true was that, because what was happening in Bosnia was genocide, most of the journalists did come to sympathize with the Bosnian cause, in exactly the way one hopes that if representatives of the foreign press had been stationed in the Warsaw ghetto in 1943, they would have sympathized with the Jews. The logic of the United Nations' position in Bosnia seemed to suggest that had the UN existed during the Second World War, and thought it had been given a "mandate" to treat all sides impartially, it might have complained that the journalists were failing to understand that anti-Semitism was a centuries-old European problem, and that the anxieties of the Germans about Jewish influence had to be understood in their historical context. From a strictly historical standpoint, it happens that those things were true then, just as historical explanations of Serb nationalism were true in 1994. But the press, to its credit, did not accept the UN's gloss on the old French saying that to understand everything is to forgive everything. In Bosnia, reporters had seen things that they could not forgive, things UN people had seemed hell-bent to go to any lengths to cover up.

Media Propaganda

Phillip Corwin

The United Nations sent a peacekeeping force—called the
United Nations Protection Force (UNPROFOR)—to Bosnia
when war broke out in 1992. The UN mandate was to remain
neutral in order to broker a cease-fire agreement between the
Serbs, Croats, and Muslims. During the first months of the
war, Bosnians looked to UNPROFOR soldiers as their sav-
iors. UNPROFOR brought food into the besieged city of
Sarajevo, for example, and arranged to have injured children
airlifted out. However, as the war dragged on and the deaths
mounted, Bosnians began to blame the peacekeepers for not
acting to end the siege of Sarajevo and stop the war. The
international media sided with the Bosnian government and
began to accuse the Bosnian Serb Army of starting the war
and committing genocide. The media also began to criticize
the United Nations for its neutral mandate, which they
believed was helping lengthen the war.

Phillip Corwin, a member of the UN peacekeeping force in
Sarajevo, recounts his experiences with the international
media. In his diary, which he kept during the summer of
1995, Corwin describes how members of the press badgered
and belittled him because he was a UN official. He claims
that the media bias toward the Bosnian government was illogical and amounted to propaganda. Phillip Corwin has held a
variety of posts for the United Nations in a career spanning
over twenty-seven years.

*Editor's Note: The author made additional comments in his di-
ary after it was written. He has used brackets to differentiate these
additions from the original material.*

From *Dubious Mandate: A Memoir of the UN in Bosnia, Summer 1995*, by Phillip Corwin.
Copyright © 1999, Duke University Press. All rights reserved. Reprinted with permission.

19 June 1995

At breakfast this morning, Alex Ivanko, the Civil Affairs spokesman, asked me if I would like to attend the noon press conference today. There are daily press briefings at the Sarajevo airport. UNPROFOR has one civilian spokesman, Ivanko, and one British military spokesman, Lt. Col. Gary Coward. Because I went to Pale [the seat of the Serb-controlled area of Bosnia] recently, and because I am fairly new on the job, the press are interested in speaking to me. After some hesitation, I agreed to go to the press conference.

[Among ourselves (at the United Nations), we referred to the press as reptiles. We called them the International Order of Reptiles—the IOE. In fact, there were times when it seemed one needed a Ph.D. in herpitology to deal with these self-appointed chroniclers of history.

The main problem for the UN with the press was that they hated us. The main problem for me was that I often lost patience with their hating us. Unfortunately, a strange logic prevailed when dealing with the Reptiles. If you endured their abuse, then you were "good" with the press, but if you dared to question their hegemony and misinformation, then you didn't know how to handle the press.

Smith was much better and much shrewder with the media than I was. He took them in small doses, one or two at a time, over dinner or in his office, but he never faced the wolf pack en masse, even though they liked him. I was both foolish and arrogant in thinking I could debate them, perhaps even win them over to some objectivity. No way. They were a clenched fist, always looking for new ways to pummel UNPROFOR.]

The Kennel

Walking into a press conference at the Sarajevo airport is like entering a kennel. Today in particular the press was legion. I have no idea what the advance word on me was, but it didn't much matter. UNPROFOR, especially [under-Secretary-General of the United Nations Yasushi] Akashi and his personal representative, are considered villains and have to be excoriated at every opportunity. The facts are irrelevant, the personalities are insignificant. Nominally, my reason for being there was to speak about the prospects for restoring utilities to Sarajevo.

I made an opening statement saying that I had presented to both sides a proposal for restoring utilities to Sarajevo and that I was awaiting a response. The proposal was nonpolitical. It spoke about who would turn on what, in which order, and when.

The audience was outraged. It wasn't clear why, but they were outraged. One reporter asked how I could have dared to go to Pale to speak with the Serbs when only yesterday they had shelled Sarajevo, killing innocent people who were standing in line at a water pump. Children had been among the victims. Wasn't I rewarding terrorism by going to Pale the very next day?

I had gone to Pale only to present the Serbs with a text of the possible steps for restoring utilities to Sarajevo, I said. I repeated that the text simply said who would turn on what and where and in which order. It was purely a technical text, with no political message whatsoever. I was hopeful.

"What was the problem?" the *New York Times* reporter asked.

"There was no problem," I said. I had presented a text and was awaiting an answer. I had presented it only yesterday, so it was too soon to expect a decision.

Meet the Press

Then a reporter from one of the American TV networks screamed (yes, screamed) at me. I wasn't quite sure what he was asking because it was more a performance than a question, but generally he was asking the same question that the previous reporter asked. How could I speak to those terrorists in Pale about restoring utilities when they had only yesterday massacred innocent children in Sarajevo, while the UN had done nothing to retaliate? If the Serbs had not turned off the water in the first place, then there wouldn't have been a line at the water pump and *innocent children* (he liked that phrase) wouldn't have been slaughtered while the UN looked on indifferently. Or something like that. The query was almost incoherent. He was so righteously indignant that he could scarcely spit out the words. Of course, what he wanted was to antagonize me in order to embarrass the UN and to get a good sound bite. Never mind that the Serbs are *not* solely responsible for turning off the water. Never mind that the UN is *not* indifferent to the slaughter of children. Never mind that the Serbs did not turn off the water *in order to kill children standing in line at a water pump.* And so forth. The facts don't matter.

But stupidly I lost my temper. Perhaps the screaming even more than the incoherence set me off. I wanted to tell him that his tone confirmed the fact that hysteria is not gender specific, but I didn't say that. What I *did* say, however, was even worse: "That question is so illogical that I won't even dignify it with an answer."

The Rattlesnake

I had swallowed the bait. An audible round of "oohs" went through the kennel. A moment later, the Reuters reporter asked me a contrived question that invited me to denounce the barbaric Serbs. I smiled, having anticipated the question. [I was certainly not sympathetic to the Bosnian Serb Army's (BSA) shelling of civilian targets in Sarajevo, but I was not eager to denounce publicly, except in the most general terms, a party I was dealing with and from which I was seeking compliance. Why, I wondered, couldn't he ask an intelligent question, instead of being so predictable?] He immediately picked up on my smile and demanded to know why I was smiling. "Perhaps you can share with us why you're smiling so that you can amuse us, too. Come on, amuse us."

What I wanted to reply was that he, being past puberty, should have known by now how to amuse himself, but with great restraint, I didn't say that. Instead, I dodged the question and mumbled something about only wanting to help the people of Sarajevo by restoring utilities to the city. I was simply astonished by the personal abuse aimed at me and the institutional hatred against the UN.

The conference went on for another fifteen minutes or so, along the same confrontational lines. Once or twice our spokesmen intervened to protect me, but the judgment had already been made. The UN had been proven guilty, beyond a reasonable doubt, of not toeing the politically correct line.

I lost a key battle, and it was my fault. One cannot blame a rattlesnake for being a rattlesnake. It was my responsibility to deal intelligently with the press, and I did not.

[A few days later I received a call from New York, advising me to be more careful with the press in future. The stories about my press conference had gone out and had been monitored at UN headquarters in New York. Because I didn't see any of the reports myself, I can't say firsthand exactly how I was skewered, but I was sure the summaries were nasty.

One publication that was particularly spiteful toward the United Nations and me personally during the time I was in former Yugoslavia, in Croatia as well as in Bosnia, was the *Christian Science Monitor.* Its main reporter, David Rohde, was an ambitious, peripatetic opportunist who was passionately pro-Bosnian. . . .

In contrast to the *Christian Science Monitor,* I thought that *The Washington Post* was more balanced, though certainly not sympathetic to the Serbs. Their correspondent, John Pomfret, made an effort to ferret out the complexities of the story. Of course, the *Post* followed the approved line when dealing with Bosnia, but at least Pomfret did not adhere to the ban on criticizing the Bosnian government. As for CNN's First Lady of Bosnia, Christiana Amanpur . . . she made no pretense of being objective. She was fond of telling anyone who wanted to listen that to be objective in Bosnia was to be a party to genocide. In my faxes I used to refer to CNN as *C*ertainly *N*ot *N*eutral.]

God's Agents

There are numerous British journalists here, and perhaps because I am English speaking, I overestimate their influence.

Yet they seem to give a character to the mission. They are, with few exceptions (such as Laura Silber), highly sanctimonious and culturally condescending. They are among the most hypocritical and supercilious, and seem to assume that they were chosen by God to assist the suffering and that in some way the Americans and the French, for different reasons, are responsible for whatever ills exist in the present situation.

Naturally, one always wants to assist those who are suffering, and it is very noble to do so, but it is the attitude that they are God's agents on earth that I find so offensive.

One female journalist keeps telling me about how *we* have to promote multiethnic democracy—the most advanced form of society—how the Bosnian government is the only party pursuing that path, and how *we,* therefore, have to support them.

Wrong, I say. Former Yugoslavia was a multiethnic society before republics like Bosnia began seceding. Now none of the warring parties believes in multiethnicity.

Besides, what right does perfidious Albion [Britain] have to impose its view of Western values on the people of the Balkans and to suggest they are backward if they don't see history through British eyes? This approach is the worst form of racism and not inconsistent with a certain element in British society. The sad truth is that many people in the Balkans prefer to live among their own kind. To many in the West, including myself, such provincial behavior is puzzling. Yet, it should not be considered immoral or uncivilized. At the same time, wanting to be among your own kind does not mean you should slaughter those *not* of your kind.

Another journalist, a female in her twenties from a prominent London daily, is fond of telling me how she, having spent ten months in Sarajevo, considers herself to be a Sarajevan. "We are all Sarajevans," she insists. (*We?* The international press? Unlike me, of course, a mongrel American and a UN official.) Never mind that she can, whenever she wishes, return to London or vacation in the South Seas, an option not available to most Sarajevans, especially the refugees. But *she* is a Sarajevan. Meanwhile, in the course of her homily she asks me when I think the Americans might agree to placing troops on the ground in Bosnia. "When they go completely out of their mind," I reply.

Clearly, I am not to be trusted.

Media Propaganda

My press conference was a disaster. It left me feeling demeaned, actively disliked, and isolated. I felt like a target, a political leper. I realize this statement sounds paranoid, but even the medical books must make allowance for a condition that might be known as "realistic paranoia." The fact is that the prevailing attitudes in Sarajevo are so cliquish, so narrow, and so prescribed that any deviation from the norm or suspected deviation from the norm is severely punished.

I also felt angry. That the Bosnian government is totalitarian in the best of Communist tradition is not even questioned by its most fervent supporters, but the accepted rationalization for this attitude is that because this is wartime, there is no room for dissent; besides, the Bosnian government is allegedly multiethnic (a key buzzword), and Sarajevo is under siege because the UN refuses to liberate it.

That a government at war should promote this line of thought is perfectly understandable, but that the international community, led by the juggernaut of the press, should voluntarily accept, promote, and attempt to impose this view on others under pain of being cast into the outer darkness is something I can never accept.

Why Would Serb Radio Lie?

Peter Maass

When the Bosnian Serb Army conquered a Bosnian village, it would "cleanse" from it all Muslim inhabitants. Serb soldiers would force the Muslims from their homes and either kill them or relocate them to concentration camps. Serb residents who remained in the village were then encouraged to take over the houses and apartments of the cleansed residents. In order to gain support for the cleansing, the Bosnian Serb Army frequently used radio broadcasts to tell fellow Serbs living in Bosnian villages that their Muslim neighbors posed a threat to them.

In the following excerpt from his book, *Love Thy Neighbor*, *Washington Post* staff writer and acclaimed foreign correspondent Peter Maass recalls an interview he had with two Serbian women living in the Bosnian town of Banja Luka. The mother and daughter had recently taken over an apartment that had been cleansed of its Muslim inhabitants. Maass describes how the unsophisticated women believed everything that the Serb military said over the radio. When radio accounts claimed that Muslims wanted to take over her village, for example, the daughter had felt relieved when her Muslim neighbors were cleansed from the village.

Vera and Stana Milanovic had no idea that their minds had been poisoned. They were Serbs who had been forced out of their homes by fighting in central Bosnia. They made their way to Banja Luka, where a relative lived, and

From *Love Thy Neighbor*, by Peter Maass. Copyright © 1996 by Peter Maass. Used by permission of Alfred A. Knopf, a division of Random House, Inc.

took over a vacant apartment. It happened like this: A few days after a family had been cleansed out of Banja Luka, Stana borrowed a crowbar and broke into the apartment. She was Serb, and her three children needed a decent roof over their heads. The toys that they found in the apartment were an unexpected bonus.

The Rationalization of Living Space

At least the flat was uninhabited when she moved in. Serbs occasionally barged into houses before the Bosnian owners had moved out. A Serb who wanted a better apartment, or a Serb family whose house was destroyed in fighting, would bang on the front door and tell the owners that the living room and kitchen no longer belonged to them. The Serbs would troop in, armed, and a week later suggest that the owners move out of the rest of the house, or else. It had a legal veneer because an old and forgotten municipal code in Banja Luka limited the apartment space that a family could have. The limit was minuscule by modern standards, which made it perfect for use against non-Serbs. This trick was known as the "rationalization of living space."

Stana opened the door a crack when I knocked, afraid that I might be an angry relative of the cleansed owners. Warily, she let me in and showed the way to the living room. The door shut behind me and, because the lock had been busted by her crowbar, she secured the door with a padlock. The sofa was covered in what seemed to be the same white shag carpeting that was on the floor. The wallpaper was pimpled with rectangular spots, reminders of the family pictures that used to hang there. The electricity was out, so Stana served water in small coffee cups, explaining that the previous occupants must have sold off the large glasses before leaving.

Her mother, Vera, a peasant woman as big as a haystack, sat next to me. It was a hot day, so she wiped the sweat from her brow with a handkerchief and then blew her nose into the same handkerchief. I sensed that, if I stayed long enough, I would likely see the same performance in reverse order.

Bogdan [my interpreter] pulled out the Marlboros

[which helped you make friends in Bosnia]. Mother and daughter beamed.

Stana had been the first to hit the road. After her village was caught up in the war, she fled to her mother's village on Vlasic Mountain, overlooking Travnik. But the fighting branched out and threatened the mother's village, too, so Vera joined her daughter in an exodus to Banja Luka. Vera said it was a pity they had to leave. Her village, after all, had been cleansed of its Muslims in the first days of the war.

Television Virus

The former Yugoslavia was a communist country and there-fore did not have freedom of the press. Indeed, Yugoslav lead-ers viewed the media as a vehicle for garnering support for government policies and officials. The majority of journal-ists belonged to the Communist Party, and any reporter who wrote criticisms of the government was immediately fired.

In the following excerpt from his book Origins of a Cata-strophe, *United States ambassador to Yugoslavia from 1989 to 1992 Warren Zimmermann explains how Yugoslav politi-cians used the media to gain support for their nationalist agendas which inevitably led to the breakup of Yugoslavia and the Bosnian war.*

Why did so many Serbs, Croats, and (later) Muslims succumb to . . . racist appeals? One function of demo-cratic government is to protect an open competition of ideas that will, it can be hoped, offset the spread of hatred. When government assumes precisely the opposite role—when it uses its power over the mass media to exhort people to hate—then many citizens look to the press not for informa-tion but for emotional reassurance. They can take righteous satisfaction in discharging their anger at their neighbors.

Even more important was the fear factor. The nationalist media sought to terrify by evoking mass murderers of a by-gone time. The Croatian press described Serbs as "Cetniks"—the Serbian nationalists of World War II. For the Serbian press Croatians were "Ustase" [Croats who helped the Nazis

The Harem Reports

I asked, out of politeness, whether the fighting in the village was heavy.

"Why, no, there was no fighting between Muslims and Serbs in the village," she said.

"Then why were the Muslims arrested?"

"Because they were planning to take over the village. They had already drawn up lists. The names of the Serb women had been split into harems for the Muslim men."

against the Serbs in World War II] (and later, Muslims became "Turks"). People who think they're under ethnic threat tend to seek refuge in their ethnic group. Thus did the media's terror campaign establish ethnic solidarity on the basis of an enemy to be both hated and feared. Many people in the Balkans may be weak or even bigoted, but in Yugoslavia it's their leaders who have been criminal. Milos Vasic, one of the best independent journalists in Yugoslavia, has said, "You Americans would become nationalists and racists too if your media were totally in the hands of the Ku Klux Klan."

The virus of television spread ethnic hatred like an epidemic throughout Yugoslavia, becoming even more malignant as sporadic violence turned into full-scale war. Worst of all, the virus had a temporal as well as a geographic effect. An entire generation of Serbs, Croats, and Muslims were aroused by television images to hate their neighbors. Every night for five years nearly everybody in Yugoslavia watched highly manipulated pictures of the maimed and the murdered, the cleansed and the condemned. One can imagine the enduring impression those pictures must have made on the minds of children and young adults, an impression that will last for decades and may even be transmitted by infected parents to children still unborn. It will make a long-term peace even harder to come by. The current nationalist leaders will someday be gone. But the seed they have sown, through their malevolent manipulation of information, will long survive them.

Warren Zimmermann, *Origins of a Catastrophe,* New York: Random House, 1996.

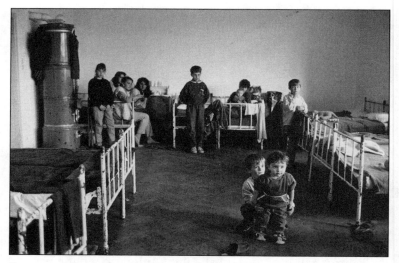

Former army barracks are used to house refugees who cannot find private accommodations.

"Harems?"

"Yes, harems. Their Bible says men can have harems, and that's what they were planning to do once they had killed our men. Thank God they were arrested first." She wiped her brow.

"How do you know they were planning to kill the Serb men and create harems for themselves?"

"It was on the radio. Our military had uncovered their plans. It was announced on the radio."

I glanced at Bogdan. Harems? Over the past few months I had heard that the Muslims would make Serb women wear chadors, the black ankle-to-head gown. I had heard that the Bosnians bombed themselves and blamed it on the Serbs. I had heard that an Islamic-Vatican-Croatian-Germanic conspiracy had been hatched to kill off the Serbs. But I had not, to date, heard anything about harems.

The look in Bogdan's eyes said, Please don't grin, because if you grin, then I'll grin, and then you'll start chuckling, and that will make me start chuckling. Bogdan knew how to keep a straight face; he learned it a few years earlier as a conscript in the Yugoslav National Army.

"How do you know the radio was telling the truth?" I asked.

Stana and Vera stared at me as though I wore no clothes. God, these Americans are dumber than cows. Vera's kindness evaporated as she flashed the kind of scowl that, I imagined, was deployed against grandchildren who wore farm boots indoors.

"Why," she demanded to know, "would the radio lie?"

I had to give up. It was the polite thing to do, even though Vera translated my silence as confirming the verity of the harem report. She took a triumphant puff on her Marlboro.

"Did any of the Muslims in your village harm you?" I asked, softly.

"No."

"Did any Muslim *ever* do anything bad to you?"

"No."

She seemed offended.

"My relations with Muslims in the village were always very good. They were very nice people."

Sarajevo Free Press

Zlatko Dizdarević

Although the Bosnian Serb Army lay siege to Sarajevo early in the war, cutting off supplies and utilities, the city's major newspaper, *Oslobodenje*, did not shut down. The newspaper's staff continued to issue the paper while the building in which they worked was being bombed. Later, when the building was consumed by fire, the staff published the paper in a modified form from other parts of the city. Throughout the siege, the *Oslobodenje* remained critical of the United Nations Peacekeeping Force, which it believed should have done more to stop the war.

Zlatko Dizdarević, a journalist for *Oslobodenje*, reports on the destruction of the *Oslobodenje* building and explains that the building was not necessary in order to publish the paper. He recounts recent deaths in Sarajevo at the hands of Bosnian Serbs, vilifies the United Nations for not acting to stop the war, and announces his paper's commitment to continue reporting the truth about the war no matter how diligently the Serbs tried to stop it.

Now [the Bosnian Serbs] imagine they've achieved their objective at last. Yesterday [June 20, 1992] the sky was in flames above Nedzarici, the district many Sarajevans know mainly by the landmark building of [the] *Oslobodenje* [newspaper]. The red sky above Nedzarici marked the demise of that great edifice, and it must have pleased the pyromaniacs of [what the United Nations calls] "one of the parties to the conflict" to no end. At the same time, however,

From *Sarajevo: A War Journal*, by Zlatko Dizdarević, published by Fromm International Publishing Corp., New York, © 1993. Reprinted with permission from the publisher.

it also confirmed a truth we have repeated many times over the last few weeks: *Oslobodenje* has emerged victorious, as it was bound to, because its existence does not depend on the building that burned, nor does it depend on the spared location, the place from which, this morning, a new issue appeared, its price doubled from yesterday's.

The [besieged] Sarajevans, many of whom are too poor to afford bread (when bread is available), bought up the entire edition in one hour. The typical reaction we heard to what had happened to us, including from some who spent the night trying to put out the fire, was, "God, it's great to know they hate you so much that they're willing to use up all that ammunition, over so many days, just to hurt you. Imagine what you must have done to them, for them to consider you so important. . . .

The Times We Live In

In other times we might have reacted differently to the fire that devoured our home. We would have grieved over the superb work spaces we had dreamt about for forty years and enjoyed for a decade. We would have talked about all the computers, all the machines and printing equipment that had remained in there and would never again be used to set a word; or we would have lamented the loss of Zuka Dzumhur's manuscripts, Adi Mulabegovic's caricatures, Mario Mikulic's and Mica Todorovic's photographs, all destroyed in the conflagration lit by imbeciles and aided by machine-gun fire whose sole purpose was to prevent us from putting it out.

But these aren't other times, these are the times we live in now. We won't weep for the building. Others more beautiful and more important already have gone up in flames. The Sarajevans are shedding tears because of what happened yesterday: The inhabitants of [the Sarajevo suburb] Dobrinja were subjected to merciless machine-gun fire by whoever had stolen some white armored vehicles belonging to the United Nations Protection Force. Those makeup artists in blue helmets didn't even bother to inform us who had stolen these vehicles, didn't even let us know that they had been stolen. Tears of rage were shed at certain words uttered by General MacKenzie, who said, imagine this, that the UN force will stop its efforts to reopen the airport unless "the two parties do not agree to a cease-fire of forty-eight hours." Further cause for tears are the dead bodies of persons killed this morning by mortar shells, in places where people have already died. Who hasn't heard about the shell that landed today on Vasa Miskin street, just like some time ago, in the middle of a breadline, hitting two mothers? What does the *Oslobodenje* building matter to children whose mothers will never return? Besides, we don't need that building now. We have our paper, and we have Sarajevo, a city that needs our paper. We are still here, safe and sound.

In the days to come, *Oslobodenje* may appear in a smaller format, and it may not have as many pages; we haven't made any final decisions about that. But there are some things that need no discussion: This paper, even if it's smaller and thinner, will go on printing everything that excites the hatred of idiots, but there will no longer be anything they could destroy. Imagine our joy! Our paper will report everything that causes that hypocrite MacKenzie as well as [Secretary-general of the United Nations Boutros-Boutros] Ghali and [under Secretary-general for political affairs Marrack] Goulding to go on fantasizing on the subject of "parties in conflict." One day, they'll be ashamed of those fantasies. As for us, we'll go on producing and preserving our paper. We'll hold on to our paper, and we'll even know how to produce reprints, to refresh the memories of those whose memories will need to be refreshed.

Chapter 5

The World's Response

Chapter Preface

After the war between the Croatian Serbs and Croatia ended in 1992 with the signing of a cease-fire agreement, the United Nations (UN) sent a peacekeeping operation to enforce peace in the area. This was a traditional UN peacekeeping operation that was designed to enforce a peace already established between parties who wanted to stop fighting. The UN operation was a neutral force charged with overseeing the cease-fire both sides had agreed to. This peacekeeping force was not originally slated to get involved in the war in Bosnia, but as fighting heated up in the newly independent state, UN forces stepped in.

Bosnian president Alija Izetbegovic had asked for UN protection immediately following Bosnia's declaration of independence in March 1992. The president feared reprisals from the Bosnian Serbs and Croats who might protest domination by Bosnia's Muslim majority. However, UN officials declined to help, arguing that the organization's purpose was not to help a province of a sovereign state secede. The UN maintained this stance until war broke out in Bosnia in the spring of 1992. In May, the UN decided to dispatch a force to assist humanitarian aid efforts in the country and to re-open the airport in Sarajevo, then under Serb control. The UN protection force in Bosnia—called UNPROFOR—operated under a mandate that required strict neutrality.

When UN peacekeepers first arrived in Bosnia, people welcomed them. Bosnians viewed them as proof that the world cared about their plight. As the war dragged on, however, Bosnian attitudes toward UNPROFOR changed. UNPROFOR's adherence to the neutrality mandate prevented them from firing on Bosnian Serbs, for example, even when the Serbs were massacring thousands of civilians in Sarajevo. International journalists in Bosnia began to vilify UNPRO-

FOR for not doing more to protect civilians and punish the Serbs, who they considered the aggressors. In spite of unceasing criticism, UNPROFOR remained in Bosnia throughout the war. Its leaders defended its policy of nonaggression and claimed credit for helping to create the success of the Dayton Accords, which ended the war in November 1995.

The role that UNPROFOR played in the Bosnian war was the source of much contention. Many critics argue that UNPROFOR symbolized the West's failure to do anything to prevent or end the war. There is little doubt that UNPROFOR's ambiguous role in Bosnia underscores the ambivalence with which the West viewed its own responsibility to help end the Balkan tragedy.

Failing to Avert Disaster

Richard Holbrooke

Europe and the United States were reluctant to get involved in the Balkans even while rumors of war reached them. Europe did not believe that the break-up of Yugoslavia was a real threat to stability in the region, while the United States was reluctant to get involved in what it viewed as a messy civil war. In addition, the United States was less interested in helping communist Yugoslavia once the Cold War—and the threat of Soviet-style communism—had ended.

Richard Holbrooke, the U.S. assistant secretary of state for European and Canadian affairs from 1994 to 1996 and the chief architect for the 1995 Dayton Peace Accords, argued as early as 1992 that the United States should get more involved in the conflict in Bosnia. In the following excerpt from his book *To End a War*, Holbrooke describes the chaos he witnessed as he traveled through Bosnia as a private citizen. In journal entries and excerpts from memoranda and articles, he recounts his attempts to get the United States government to bomb the Serbs or help supply the Muslims with weapons. According to Holbrooke, the United States' refusal to take timely action in Bosnia contributed to the death and destruction that followed.

August 13, 1992

After a day of briefings in Zagreb, [in Croatia] I can see that the situation [in Bosnia] is far more complicated and more difficult

From *To End a War,* by Richard Holbrooke. Copyright © 1998 by Richard Holbrooke. Used by permission of Random House, Inc.

than other problems I have seen, even Cambodia. It is the peculiar three-sided nature of the struggle here that makes it so difficult. Everyone says that most people did not want this to happen. Yet it did. Everyone says it must stop. Yet it doesn't.

The U.N. refugee briefing yesterday was depressing. Maps filled with the numbers of refugees in each sector lined the room. Our host, Tony Land, a bearded Englishman with a wry sense of humor and a keen sense of the impossibility of his task, gave us a fine explanation of the situation. But when we ask him about the prison camps, he surprises us. "We are absolutely amazed at the press and public reaction to all this," he says. "For six months we have seen Sarajevo systematically being destroyed without the world getting very upset. Now a few pictures of people being held behind barbed wire, and the world goes crazy. We have seen more deaths in Sarajevo than in the prisons . . ."

This turns out to be a widely shared view among the international fieldworkers. On one hand, they are right—the war is deadlier than the camps. But to the extent that television pictures rouse the world to attention and action—they are, for example, the reason we [Americans] are here—the pictures of the camps will help Land do his job. . . .

Noon: The difficult trip to Banja Luka [in Bosnia] has begun. As I write this, we are sitting in a long line of cars and trucks at the Croatian border, about 60 kilometers from Banja Luka, on the edge of the "Serbian Republic of Krajina"—the Serb-controlled areas of western Croatia. The town just ahead of us has life in it, but an air of tension—little sound, no one raises their voices. A moment ago we heard machine gun fire, and smoke is rising in the near distance. Our driver has just nervously asked me to stop videotaping from our car window. The mood is subdued and edgy.

Five P.M.: We have arrived in Banja Luka after a trip across land wasted by war. There is no electricity in the town. Our rooms at the Hotel Bosna are small and hot. Heavy gunfire breaks out just outside the hotel. No one can see where it is coming from, and in the street people keep going, on bike or foot, as though nothing has happened.

Later: The afternoon begins with a scary incident—I am hauled out of my hotel room by Serb policemen because someone reported that I had illegally videotaped inside the U.N. warehouse. Stalling in my room for a moment, I quickly erase the offending footage and go with a young U.N. employee to see a Serb security officer at the warehouse. Our interpreter-guide explains to the nasty-looking Serb security man that I am not a journalist, etc., and after an angry talk, everything seemed to be under control.

Our young guide illustrates the dilemma here. When I ask him what his background is, he says, "I don't know what I am." He goes on to explain that his immediate family (parents, in-laws, grandparents) is a mixture of Croatian, Serb, Armenian, Russian, Muslim, and Slovenian. "What can I do?" he asks. "I have three choices: to leave, to join the army, or to help people. I choose the third—for now . . . ."

August 14

An extraordinary day! It begins with loud noise and shooting outside our hotel rooms. We go outside to find armed Serbs conducting a "mild" form of ethnic cleansing right in front of journalists with television cameras. We tape the whole scene. At close to gunpoint, Muslims are signing papers giving up their personal property, either to neighbors or in exchange for the right to leave Bosnia. Then they are herded onto buses headed for the border, although they have no guarantee they will actually be able to leave the country. Some leave quietly, others crying. This is the end of their lives in an area their families have lived in for centuries.

After this terrible scene, which leaves us shaken and subdued, we pile into white U.N. vehicles. A few miles north of Banja Luka, we begin to see terrible signs of war—houses destroyed all along the route. As we progress toward the front lines, the destruction increases. We encounter the occasional house left completely undamaged in a row of ruined ones—its occupant a Serb, not a Muslim. Such destruction is clearly not the result of fighting, but of a systematic and methodical pogrom in which Serbs fingered their Muslim neighbors. This is how it must have been in Central Europe and Russia a century ago, but now using modern weapons and communications.

We are guided through this horrorscape by a tiny and vivacious young Montenegrin from the U.N. named Senja, who spent a year in Ft. Collins, Colorado, as an exchange student. Whenever we hit a roadblock, she firmly orders us to stay in the car and take no pictures. Then she hops out to talk our way past the awful-looking guards, lounging around with their weapons.

The men in this country act as if they would be impotent if they didn't carry guns. Weapons have empowered people who were until recently gas station mechanics or shopkeepers. I have never seen so many weapons on so many men, even in Vietnam and Cambodia.

We drive to Sanski Most, crossing a difficult checkpoint at a bridge. As we reach the local Red Cross offices, the most frightening incident of the day occurs: an angry-looking man in a sloppy uniform, wearing Reeboks and smoking a cigarette, starts yelling and waving a semi-automatic around wildly in our direction. He seems drunk. He wants to "borrow" our vehicle, then dump us at the edge of the town—or worse. After a heated argument, Senja insists we be taken to the local police station, where she tells us to stay outside while she goes in alone. For a tense hour we wait, watched with open hostility by the heavily armed men lounging in front of the police station. We worry about Senja, but finally she emerges from the police station, saying urgently, "We have to leave immediately. These people are very angry and very dangerous." And we take off rapidly for Zagreb, relieved but mystified. . . .

August 15

We have flown to Split [in Croatia]. After checking in at a lovely resort hotel on the sea, we set out for a refugee holding area just across the Croatian border in Bosnia, climbing through a typical Mediterranean landscape, with steep rocky mountains. seaside houses, and small villages. The towns could be in Italy, just across the Adriatic, but the militia makes me think more of Lebanon.

We arrive in Posesje, a town just inside the Bosnian border. The refugee holding area is a dreadful mess. In a school and its grounds are about 3,000 Muslim refugees who have fled from Serb-controlled areas of Bosnia and were stopped by the Croatians from crossing the border into Croatia.

Under a broiling sun, with several women crying out their stories at the same time, the refugees tell us for hours of the ordeals they and their families have lived through. Women gather around to recount how their men are still missing, how they were taken away and never seen again. No young men around. It is overwhelmingly oppressive. We return, depleted, to Split.

For a change of pace, we go to the ancient Roman ruins, near the main street. At this time of year Split is usually filled with tourists, but now there are only a few, mostly German, who seem a dreadful, walking insult to the terrible events happening a few miles away. We visit Emperor Diocletian's palace, a small part of which has been converted into a church.

As we look around, an unforgettable scene takes place, in sharp contrast to the rest of the day. Two nuns appear and sit down at the organ. A young girl starts singing, rehearsing for a wedding. Her beautiful voice fills the little church, echoing off the ancient stones. We stop, transfixed. The horrors of Bosnia are both far away and

---

A Sentence of Death

Due to a United Nations arms embargo against Yugoslavia in 1991, Bosnian Muslims were at a decided disadvantage. Even though the UN recognized Bosnia as an independent nation in 1992, it continued to apply the arms embargo against it, and the Muslims had to obtain their arms from Islamic nations such as Iran. On the other hand, the Bosnian Serbs had plenty of weapons. Noel Malcolm, a political columnist for London's Daily Telegraph, *who covered the Balkans for fifteen years, explains in the following excerpt from his book* Bosnia: A Short History *that the Bosnian Serbs had help from Serbia. Malcolm argues that the West's arms embargo ensured the destruction of Bosnia.*

Because the war was seen essentially as a military problem—caused by a thing called 'violence' which had 'flared up' on 'both sides'—the efforts of the West were directed at what was described as 'reducing the quantity of fighting'. Hence the biggest single contribution by the West to the destruction of Bosnia: the refusal to lift the arms em-

yet right here. We cannot tear ourselves away. If these moments of love, family, and tradition could last longer, perhaps they could fill the space that war possesses in this self-destructive land.

August 16

Zagreb. Dinner is again at the buffet of the Inter-Continental, where we are joined by Steve Engelberg, an impressive *New York Times* correspondent. He offers some opinions: those who might replace [Serbia's president Slobodan] Milosevic would probably be worse; [former Secretary of State under President Jimmy Carter and foreign diplomat Cyrus] Vance did a terrific job stopping the Croatian-Serbian war; there is a serious danger of a European Islamic radical movement if this war is not stopped soon.

New York: August 23, 1992

The trip is over. As always, New York's problems are so demanding that it is hard to get people to worry about misery thousands of miles away. But I do not agree with the argument that we can-

bargo against the Bosnian government. This embargo had been introduced by the UN in September 1991 against the whole of Yugoslavia, which at that stage was still, formally speaking, a single country. Although the UN itself recognized Bosnia and admitted it as a member-state distinct and separate from Yugoslavia on 22 May 1992, it continued to apply the embargo as if nothing had changed. Of course it continued to apply it to Serbia too; but Serbia held most of the stockpiles of the former federal army, and had a large armaments industry of its own. . . . In addition, the Yugoslav army had purchased an extra 14,000 tons of weaponry from the Middle East just before the arms embargo came into force in 1991. Serb military commanders sometimes boasted that they had enough arms and ammunition to continue the war in Bosnia for another six or seven years; the embargo could have no real effect on their military capability. But to the Bosnian defence forces it was in the long term a sentence of death.

Noel Malcolm, *Bosnia: A Short History*. New York: New York University Press, 1996.

not afford to deal with these faraway problems when we have difficulties at home. Such thinking leads to an unacceptable global triage. Our society is still rich enough to deal with the outside world, even after the end of the Cold War.

The trip had hooked me. Not since Vietnam had I seen a problem so difficult or compelling. I told Strobe Talbott, then a columnist at *Time,* that if there were a change in Administrations Bosnia would be "the worst kind of legacy imaginable—it would be [President] George Bush and [Bush's Secretary of State] Larry Eagleburger's revenge if [Bill] Clinton wins [the presidency]." Before the trip, *The Washington Post* and *Newsweek* had both asked me to write about my trip. I was now anxious to do so. The *Newsweek* article, in the issue of September 17, 1992, marked my first effort to propose a course of action in Bosnia:

> By its inadequate reaction so far, the United States and, to an even greater extent, the European Community may be undermining not only the dreams of a post-Cold War "common European House" but also laying the seeds for another era of tragedy in Europe.
>
> Not that such a dire future is inevitable. . . . If the Europeans and the United States act with boldness and strength, worst-case scenarios do not need to occur. . . . [But] if the war continues, and the Serbs succeed in permanently reducing the Muslims to a small state or "cantonment" within a Bosnia that has been divided between Croatia and Serbia, the immediate consequences will be terrible—and the long-term consequences even worse. In the short run, the Muslims will have been removed from areas in which they have lived for centuries, with countless thousands butchered, often by their longtime neighbors. Hundreds of thousands, perhaps over one million refugees will have been thrust into a world community already staggering under enormous refugee burdens in Africa, Southeast Asia, and South Asia. . . . Most observers believe that nothing is likely to deter the Serbs except actions that raise the costs of their genocidal policies to an unacceptable level.
>
> What might this mean in practice? First, international (presumably United Nations) observers should be deployed along the borders and in Kosovo and Macedonia immediately, *before* fighting

spreads to these two critical regions. . . .

Another possibility would be to change the rules of the present embargo on all combatants—which in practice heavily favors the Serbs, who control the old Yugoslav military-industrial complex—so that the Bosnians can obtain more weapons with which to defend themselves. . . .

Other actions, including bombing the bridges linking Serbia with Bosnia and attacking Serb military facilities, must be considered. Such actions may well increase the level of violence in the short term. But since the West does not intend or wish to send its own troops into the war, it is unfair to deny the Muslims the means with which to defend themselves. . . .

Every day that the killing goes on the chances of preventing the long-term tragedy decrease. What would the West be doing now if the religious convictions of the combatants were reversed, and a Muslim force was now trying to destroy two million beleaguered Christians and/or Jews? . . .

The 1993 Memorandum

On January 13, 1993, one week before they were to assume office, I sent a long memorandum to [Secretary of State] Warren Christopher and [National Security Adviser] Tony Lake. It began:

> Bosnia will be the key test of American policy in Europe. We must therefore succeed in whatever we attempt. The Administration cannot afford to begin with either an international disaster or a quagmire. Despite the difficulties and risks involved, I believe that inaction or a continuation of the Bush policies in Bosnia by the Clinton Administration is the least desirable course. Continued inaction carries long-term risks which could be disruptive to U.S.-European relations, weaken the North Atlantic Treaty Organization (NATO), increase tension in Greece and Turkey, and cause havoc with Moscow. . . .

> No one with whom I talked last August expected the Bosnians to last this long. . . . An important reason the Bosnian Muslims are surviving is that they are beginning to get significant weapons ship-

ments from Islamic nations, apparently including Iran. These are coming through Croatia, *with Croatian complicity.* . . . Four key points about these *not-so-secret* secret shipments to the Muslims:

—first, the Croats, who do not want to let the Muslims become too strong, have not allowed them to include heavy weapons or artillery;

—second, every weapons shipments has a Croatian "weapons tax"; that is, the Croats siphon off some of the weapons for their own army and for the HVO [the Bosnian Croats] in Bosnia-Herzegovina;

—third, there is now strong evidence that small but growing numbers of "freedom fighters" or mujahideen are joining the Bosnian forces, although, as one might expect, the strict fundamentalists from the Mideast and the loose, secular Muslims of Bosnia do not understand each other or mix well;

—finally, these shipments will continue—and they will increase.

I suggested four objectives for the new Administration: first, "to save as many lives as possible in Bosnia"; second, "to make containment of the war a top priority"; third, "to punish the Serbs for their behavior . . . and to brand certain individuals war criminals"; fourth, "to use this crisis as an opportunity to strengthen the U.N. system." We should act, I added, "in concert with other nations," even creating "some sort of ad hoc military coalition, [but] avoid getting dragged into a ground war in the region."

At the time the incoming Administration was trying to decide whether to support peace proposals put forward by Cyrus Vance and David Owen, the former British Foreign Secretary who had replaced Lord Carrington as the European Union negotiator. The Vance-Owen plan proposed dividing Bosnia into ten "cantons," some of which would be Muslim-controlled, some Serb-controlled, and some Croat-controlled. It had been attacked by many American commentators as a sellout, another Munich, and a precursor to the breakup of Bosnia.

There was already deep division within the new team about Bosnia. The Joint Chiefs of Staff, led by its formidable Chairman, Colin Powell, was especially opposed to American involvement. The Vance-Owen plan was flawed, but if the United States killed it without coming up with a plan of its own, the consequences would be far worse, so I recommended that Washington give qualified public support to their plan:

> If Vance-Owen leads to a temporary cessation of fighting and relief to the Muslims, and offers the new Administration some breathing room to put a [full-fledged] policy into place, it should be welcomed. It will not solve the problem, only perhaps let the world think it is solved for a while. If the Vance-Owen plan is rejected, we must face the fact that the negotiating track is effectively dead—and that using it as an excuse for inaction or insufficient action is no longer acceptable.

I ended the memorandum with a series of specific recommendations, actions that the United States should consider, especially if the Vance-Owen plan was either rejected or if it failed. This was the most provocative part of the paper:

> *Lifting the Arms Embargo to Bosnia:* I favored lifting the arms embargo to the Bosnians, before I visited the region, and am still in favor of it, if it can gain U.N. Security Council approval. But this might be difficult to obtain (and create strains with Moscow). . . .

I would therefore [also] recommend consideration of something that I know will cause many people heartburn: that we allow covert arms supply to the Bosnian Muslims, *so that Bosnia's outside support no longer comes solely from the Islamic Nations.* Such a policy requires sophistication within the U.S. Government (USG), including Congress, and, if it involves the US directly, a legal finding. It would undoubtedly leak, as our support to the Afghan resistance leaked long before it was openly acknowledged. But this might be the best way to help the Bosnians quickly without provoking a new round of escalatory steps from the Serbs. It does, however, carry the serious drawback of showing the United States evading a Security Council resolution that it previously supported. This concern could be lessened if our actions were accompanied by public efforts at the U.N. to change the embargo, or if *we acted only through third parties,* as we did in Afghanistan.

Direct Use of Force Against the Serbs: Bombing the Bosnian Serbs and even Serbia proper if necessary would send the proper message. However, the actions must be effective, both militarily and politically! . . . If done only to show the world we are "doing something," minor bombing—like the enforcement of the no-fly zone—might be a quick public relations success, but it would be followed by a long-term disaster.

Establish an American Diplomatic Presence in Sarajevo: This would be a dramatic step to show the world where we stand. An American Embassy can be very small; symbolism counts.

Keep Up the Pressure on the War Criminal Issue: This policy, while belated, is useful. Name more names. Set up a separate staff to create more pressure on this front.

No one replied to this memorandum. Finally, some weeks after the Inauguration of Bill Clinton as president, I called Lake to ask if he had received it. Yes, he said, they had gotten it; it was "useful," but it contained some suggestions that would "undercut us at the U.N." We argued the issue briefly, but hopelessly.

The United States Was Wrong to Bomb the Serbs

Phillip Corwin

Bosnian Serbs reacted to Bosnia's declaration of independence from Yugoslavia in 1992 by immediately trying to partition off and control regions that were heavily populated by Serbs. With the help of the Yugoslav Army (JNA), the Bosnian Serbs managed to cleanse many regions of their Muslim inhabitants and hold the areas by force in an effort to create the Bosnian Serb Republic. Most countries in the West, including the United States, viewed these tactics as acts of aggression and condemned Serbian war crimes. In 1995, the United States decided to bomb Serbian targets in an effort to end the war.

Phillip Corwin, in the following excerpt from his book *Dubious Mandate*, argues that the United States was wrong to act with force against the Serbs without trying to understand their concerns. Corwin, a twenty-seven year veteran with the United Nations, was stationed in Bosnia during the war and talked with countless Serbs. Most of the Serbs he talked to feared the Muslim majority. They remembered that Muslims had helped the Croats and Nazis exterminate thousands of Serbs during World War II and believed that ethnic hatred against the Serbs would now resurface. In addition, Corwin explains that Serbs had been a majority in Yugoslavia and enjoyed many perquisites such as good government jobs as a result. When Bosnia seceded from Yugoslavia, however,

From *Dubious Mandate: A Memoir of the UN in Bosnia, Summer 1995*, by Phillip Corwin. Copyright © 1999, Duke University Press. All rights reserved. Reprinted with permission.

Serbs suddenly found themselves a minority and feared giving up the privileges that they were accustomed to.

Would it be too much, I wondered, to ask *why* U.S. planes are bombing Bosnian Serbs . . . ? Have we forgotten that during World War II the Serbs and the Jews and the Gypsies went to the concentration camps together, and that the Croats and the Bosnians, under Nazi tutelage, ran them? Such memories are not irrelevant. One should not be mired in history, but one cannot selectively ignore it either. Serb racism and Serb fascism in Bosnia are certainly to be condemned, but the anxieties that provoked them have legitimacy.

Legitimate Serbian Concerns

My experiences with the Serbs in the past few years have taught me that they believed Washington was more interested in Middle Eastern oil than in justice in Bosnia. In their siege mentality the Serbs believe that Moslems anywhere in the world are equated with Middle Eastern oil and that the West needs oil more than it needs Serbs. Never mind that such "logic" is illogical (or that Saudi Arabia may think the same way). Irrational anxiety is a factor in any political crisis and must be given its due.

I remain convinced that if the United States wants to see stability in Central Europe, as I believe it does, then it has to take account of the just concerns of the largest ethnic group in former Yugoslavia—namely, the Serbs. Such recognition does not imply endorsement of ethnic cleansing. It requires vision beyond the next Congressional election, however.

The Bosnian Serbs are constantly asking me why, after having been Yugoslavs for fifty years, they should suddenly, without their consent, have to become a minority in a Moslem-ruled state. When I tell them that Bosnian Moslems are neither fundamentalists nor Middle Easterners, that they eat pork and get drunk like any good European, they ask me who has the largest mission in Bosnia, who is the major arms supplier to the Bosnian government, and who extends the most financial credit to the Bosnian government. The answer to all three questions is the same: Iran. Of course, having diplomatic relations with Iran does not mean that a nation is necessarily a fundamentalist nation. Any port in a storm, so to speak. The Bosnian government goes wherever it can for aid, especially since the UN Security Council has slapped an arms embargo against all of Yugoslavia, but aid is seldom given without political strings attached. Though I never believed the Bosnian government intended to become fundamentalist, I understand why the Bosnian Serbs fear that possibility.

More to the point, I am fond of asking my European and North American (Christian and Jewish) friends who are so emotionally pro-Bosnian: if tomorrow you were told, through no decision of your own, that you were no longer a citizen of your own country, but were now a member of a minority in a Moslem country that had never before been a country, that had been a Nazi collaborator during World War II, what would you say? Without exception, they answer the equivalent of "No way!" . . .

Reprehensible Tactics, Just Concerns

The Bosnian Serbs have made two inexcusable and indefensible tactical errors: ethnic cleansing and the targeting of innocent civilians. The fact that all sides have committed these crimes does not exonerate the Bosnian Serbs, who have done it more often and more brutally. Nonetheless, one must acknowledge the legitimate anxiety of the Bosnian Serbs about having their country dismembered by the international community. They do not appreciate being told they can no longer be Yugoslavs, and that they must suddenly be ruled by a government dominated by Moslems, the descendants of those who were their enemies during World War II. *People have been known to become very angry when their country is taken away from them.* "For fifty years I was Yugoslav, and now suddenly I'm a Serb in a Moslem country," one Bosnian Serb said to me. "If Bosnia can secede from Yugoslavia, then we should be able to secede from Bosnia," Serbs say to me. What, in other words, are the limits of self-determination?

The inescapable fact is the tactics of the Bosnian Serbs are reprehensible but they do have a legitimate political concern. Had that concern been taken seriously from the start, war might have been averted; even now, taking that concern seriously might hasten an early and long-term solution. One has to distinguish causes from tactics. The Bosnian Serbs have cause to feel threatened as a minority in Bosnia.

The problem is that all throughout former Yugoslavia we have the equivalent of a kakistocracy. If, from the start, the Bosnian Serbs had had responsible leaders, those leaders would have tried to still the concerns of their people. They would have said, "Don't worry. We will have international guarantees for your rights; we will still have a major voice in the new government; we will be able to maintain our cultural institutions, our ties to Serbia. Don't panic." But instead of calming their people, the Bosnian Serb leadership inflamed them, and the leaders of other ethnic groups also inflamed their people. Historical scholars will document these inflammatory statements. They were endless, they were terribly damaging, and perhaps worst of all they obscured the legitimacy of the concerns each side had and has.

Why Germany forced recognition of the independence of the former Yugoslav republics of Slovenia and Croatia so soon will be debated for decades. Perhaps German Foreign Minister Hans-Dietrich Genscher merely wanted to flex his muscles as the premier continental power; perhaps he felt that recognition would actually *prevent* a war that seemed to be building. In any case, a Yugoslav friend once described his views on the subject to me in the following epigram: Yugoslavia never should have been divided, and Germany never should have been united.

A Threatened Minority

With the secession of Croatia and Bosnia and Herzegovina from the former Yugoslavia, the Serbs in those new states moved from being a privileged plurality to becoming a threatened minority. Serbs were about 31 percent of the population in Bosnia when Bosnia was part of former Yugoslavia. They didn't mind being a minority because they were a plurality in all of Yugoslavia. (According to the 1991 census, about ten out of twenty-two million Yugoslavs were Serbs; the next largest group was Croatians, about five million.) The Serbs had political power in former Yugoslavia. They had many, but not all, of the best municipal jobs, state housing, and high posts in the military. In Bosnia, the Moslems controlled commerce in the urban centers. In general, with several exceptions, the villages and the countryside in Bosnia were Serbian, and the cities were Moslem dominated, though ethnically diverse. That distinction actually provides a partial explanation for the vehemence of the Serbian policy of ethnic cleansing. One aspect of the civil war in Bosnia is the countryside pitted against the cities (as in the French Revolution). Country people (whether they be Laotian tribes or Hatfields and McCoys) are more clannish and more brutal than urban populations, which tend to be multiethnic and more socially integrated. During the five hundred-year Turkish occupation of Bosnia, the Serbs fled to the countryside, even to the mountain tops, to escape Turkish domination. When the current Bosnian war began, they had the high ground.

At the same time, the so-called multiethnic character of Bosnia is greatly exaggerated. Except for the major cities—Sarajevo, Banja Luka, Zenica, Tuzla, and Mostar—most villages and towns are often largely occupied by one group that comprises most of the population. Moreover, in almost all the towns, and even in the cities, including Sarajevo, the separate ethnic groups live in their own neighborhoods.

Indeed, there are historic precedents for ethnic separatism in Bosnia. The American translators of Mesa Selimovic's classic novel, *Death and the Dervish,* provide the following footnote in explaining a reference by Selimovic to life in seventeenth-century Sarajevo: "Seventeenth-century Sarajevo was divided into 104 *mahals,* of which twelve were

Christian, two were Jewish, and the rest Muslim." . . .

For Serbs, . . . the issue was survival of their culture, and the best way to ensure survival, they believed, was to link up all the Serbian territories in Bosnia and Croatia. If that meant "cleansing" non-Serbs, so be it. Logic was never a factor in Serb thinking at this point; anxiety and nightmares about the past were.

Imagine an Israeli being told that beginning tomorrow he would become a citizen of Egypt, or even worse, of Iraq. That is how Serbs feel about predominantly Moslem Bosnia. Please do not tell me such attitudes have no basis in fact. Irrational anxieties must be taken into account in any serious political analysis. Unfortunately, Western governments, led by the world press, simply treat this attitude as racist—as though five hundred years of Turkish occupation are irrelevant.

Blindness in the West

Roger Cohen

> During the Bosnian war, daily reports about conditions in
> Bosnia reached the outside world with regularity. Thousands
> of international journalists and photographers described the
> fighting, the concentration camps, the ethnic cleansing and
> the siege of Sarajevo. In addition, refugees streaming from
> the country told their stories to anyone who would listen. In
> spite of how well-informed the West was, however, the war in
> Bosnia went on for three years without military intervention
> from any Western nation.
>
> In the following excerpt from his book, *Hearts Grown Bru-
> tal*, Roger Cohen argues that the West refused to see the grav-
> ity of the Bosnian war in order to avoid having to do some-
> thing about it. Furthermore, Cohen maintains that it has
> become easy to ignore the graphic photographs taken of war-
> torn regions. He contends that contemporary global culture
> bombards people with so many images—music videos,
> advertisements, war photographs—that people cease to dis-
> tinguish between the frivolous and the grave. The apathy that
> results often causes people to ignore their ethical responsibil-
> ity to other people. Cohen was the Balkan bureau chief for
> the *New York Times* from 1994 to 1995.

The Serb bombardment of Sarajevo looked like mindless
barbarity in that, over more than three years, it took thousands of innocent lives and was a colossal public-relations disaster. In the early months of the conflict, however, it served
one important purpose. It distracted international attention

From *Hearts Grown Brutal,* by Roger Cohen. Copyright © 1998 by Roger Cohen. Used
by permission of Random House, Inc.

from the real business of the war.

That business was brutal, venal, and rural. It involved the eviction or slaughter of Muslims living in the provincial towns and villages of much of Bosnia during the spring, summer, and fall of 1992. The process had a ramshackle air. Serbian fascism was never slick or monolithic. Its uniforms never matched; its executions were on the advanced artisanal rather than the industrial scale. A ghoulish savagery rather than cold-blooded efficiency drove the boozy killing. Ears and sexual organs were sliced off; some people were beaten to death, a relatively time-consuming business. Bulldozers or ploughs rather than made-to-measure incinerators disposed of the victims. Ruthlessness was tempered by slovenliness. If the organizers of the Serb terror in Bosnia had been running the Nazi death camps they would have sold off the Zyklon B gas [used to kill the Jews] as soon as they were able to dispose of it for a profit.

Still, the solution was final enough. In a great arc from Sanski Most in northwestern Bosnia to Trebinje in the southeast the Serb terror unfurled. War, traditionally, is a term describing a conflict between armies. In this sense, the Bosnian war did not really start until after its defining horror was over.

Muslim civilians were taken from their homes, herded into concentration camps, and selectively killed. Surviving males, generally those without political influence or professional qualifications, were made to dig trenches until they dropped; they were bundled from camp to bestial camp, and, if they were lucky, or could somehow find a thousand German marks to buy their freedom, they were eventually pushed over the lines. Women, often raped, and children were also gathered in the camps. They huddled in silence on the floors of disused mining complexes, military depots, factories, stadiums, gymnasiums, schools before being prodded like recalcitrant cattle over the hills into territory controlled by the Bosnian government.

In a sharp burst of Serbian violence more than three quarters of a million Muslims were ousted from a swath of territory covering 70 percent of the country. Once the fabric of a society has been cut so comprehensively, it is virtually impossible to piece it together again. Once a crime is unpunished its effects fester. Fear takes root; divisions harden. Herein lay the essence, and the accuracy, of the Serbian calculation.

Genocide

The United Nations Convention defines genocide as certain "acts committed with intent to destroy in whole or in part a national, ethnical, racial or religious group, as such." This is a sober description of the Serbian rampage against the Muslims in the first six months of the Bosnian conflict. To avoid use of the term, or argue against its aptness, is to allow the Nazis a posthumous victory: the establishment of a proprietary right to "genocide" just because the scale of the Holocaust is unmatched.

It is also to grant the Serbs a victory. Throughout the wars of Yugoslavia's destruction, *genocide* was perhaps the most overused word in the Serbian vocabulary. The refrain of arguments emanating from Belgrade was that of the repetitive "genocide" suffered by the Serbian people—in Croatia, in Kosovo, in Bosnia, in Serbia itself. Deployed in this way, "genocide" was no longer a horror but a form of immunity. It was a *passe-partout* allowing the eternal Serbian victim to butcher with impunity.

[Serbian president Slobodan] Milosevic loved the word. At the opening of the peace conference in The Hague on September 7, 1991, he accused Croatia of "a policy of genocide." His speech to representatives of the European Union in Geneva on December 9, 1993, went even further and typified a well-honed Serbian genre. Attacking international trade sanctions on Serbia, he declared, "I do not know how you will explain to your children, on the day when they discover the truth, why you killed our children, why you led a war against three million of our children, and with what right you turned twelve million inhabitants of Europe into a test site for the application of what is, I hope, the last genocide of this century."

As Pascal Bruckner, the French sociologist, has pointed out, we are confronted by two dangers: the enshrinement of Auschwitz [where the most infamous Nazi concentration camp was located] in a place of memory so sacred that we are inured to the perhaps lesser, but nonetheless real, horrors of the late twentieth century, and, conversely, the reductio ad absurdum of *genocide* through overuse of the term to the point where "henceforth any people that has massacred or annihilated another can claim to have suffered genocide."

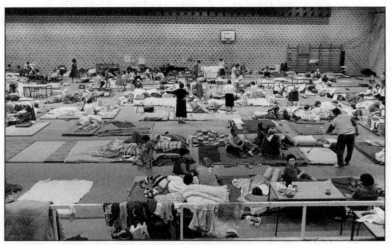

Though frequent reports of atrocities such as genocide and the emerging refugee crisis bombarded media outlets, many Western observers were unmoved by the images and tales of human suffering.

Before Our Eyes

The Bosnian genocide took place before our eyes. Many of the Serb camps were less than two hundred miles from the Austrian and Italian borders. Refugees were pouring westward with stories to tell. Reports from the International Committee of the Red Cross, survivors, and informers were reaching the [U.S.] State Department: they were not comprehensive but they painted a picture. It was summer, the skies were clear, good weather for photography. Yet, for three months, we claimed we saw nothing.

[Soviet premier from 1941 to 1953 Joseph] Stalin chose

Kolyma as the setting for one of the most savage experiments in his gulag in part because it was a very long way from anywhere. Auschwitz was a fair distance from Berlin. What happened in Bosnia therefore suggests a remarkable phenomenon: that as our capacity to see has increased to the point where any spot on the globe can be instantaneously photographed, any image instantaneously transmitted, so the necessity to conceal horror has diminished. I once pressed an American intelligence officer in Washington about this paradox. His reply was instructive. "Yes," he conceded, "in July 1992, we had pictures of Bosnia. But what is a crowd and what is a group of people about to be executed?"

Here we stand at the heart of things. *What is a crowd and what is a group of people about to be executed?* It depends, of course, on the viewer's willingness to see, capacity to discern, readiness to understand. Our age has made it easier to look without seeing. It is the age of the indifferent spectator. Useless knowledge accumulates. The Bosnian war was much looked at, little seen. It was one image amid a flood of others.

I would come away from the war with the fetid smell of misery still in my nostrils, the last knots of fear still unraveling in my gut, the last images of desolation still clutching at my mind, and find myself quite quickly in some place like Frankfurt airport looking at vending machines selling Billy Boy condoms in packages emblazoned with German blondes, and Paloma Picasso ads about how accessories are essential, and American girls with outsized backpacks complaining about their need for a shower, and brightly illuminated windows full of sophisticated alarm clocks and photographic equipment and salamis and every designer label under the sun, and I would wonder if this onslaught did not mount to the end of experience. It was not easy, in such a place, to be sentient—to remember, feel, be angry, think straight. I thought more and more about the war. I did not want it to slip from me. I did not want to be gathered back into the numbness of comfort. The more I thought about it, the more it seemed to me that, yes, Bosnia had been worth fighting for and the fascism that destroyed it worth confronting and defeating, but although the place was just a few hundred miles away, it seemed scarcely to impinge on a world in which appearance had eaten away at substance to the point where the two had become virtually indistinguishable. The most powerful images have weight; they resist the instantaneousness, and insubstantiality, of zapping. But what confronted me everywhere in our global culture was an eerie weightlessness: an R.E.M. video clip, a pile of Tutsi bodies in Rwanda (or were they Hutu?)[1], a Coca-Cola advertisement, and a woman gazing at her severed arm in Sarajevo were all part of the same undifferentiated stream. In this morass, awareness and awakening were unconnected. Life and death, right and wrong, had become disembodied issues, matters of indifference, no more than questions of management.

Managing Bosnia, for the Bush and then the Clinton administrations, meant staying out of it. That, in turn, meant a refusal to see, or acknowledge, the true gravity of the war. Its gravity—as opposed to its importance—lay precisely in the fact that the issues it raised were not primarily economic or strategic. They were moral.

Learning Not to See

The cold war victory was framed in moral terms, suggesting that it amounted to more than an opportunity to mall Central and Eastern Europe. It was about freedom overcoming walls, dignity oppression. It was, in a broad sense, about America. It was an American victory, fought for and won by Americans, for what America represents. After Bosnia, however, these truisms began to ring hollow. That summer of 1992, in the villages and small towns of Bosnia, a crowd and a group of people waiting to be executed were generally synonymous. But nobody wanted to see the photographs, listen to the fragments of testimony, piece together the manifold horror.

Ron Neitzke, an American diplomat still trying to recover

---

1. The Rwandan Armed Forces and Hutu militia have killed thousands of Tutsis in what critics in the west have called genocide.

from the way Bosnia shattered his life, said to me, "There were photographs. We [Americans] had them in 1992. If you looked you could see a little outbuilding suddenly blimping into a circus full of people. You would have reports, perhaps fragmentary, about a concentration camp at site X, and it would have been possible to look at site X and see. Somebody simply had to collate the fragmentary evidence from refugees and intercepts with the photographs. But we were determined not to see it because all this could lead to pressure for intervention. *We are learning not to see.* If a human crisis looms that we do not want to face, we withdraw resources. During the cold war, for forty-five years, we obsessed about Yugoslavia. It was one of the top three potential tinderboxes for World War III. The resources focused on that country were enormous. It was not a technical screwup that we did not see the camps. This was willed.

Preserving Peace Was the Right Thing to Do

Bill Clinton

After the 1995 Dayton Peace Accords ended the war in Bosnia, the United States pledged 20,000 troops as part of an international peacekeeping force (IFOR) in the Balkans. Many Americans—who argued that the United States should not get involved in foreign wars—had opposed U.S. participation in the North Atlantic Treaty Organization's airstrikes that had helped end the war. When Clinton asked for further U.S. involvement after the war, these critics spoke out against committing U.S. soldiers to the peacekeeping mission. Nevertheless, President Bill Clinton was successful in getting Congress to commit American troops in Bosnia.

In the following speech, Clinton outlines the reasons he believed the United States should help preserve peace in Bosnia. He argues that the United States was founded on the idea of life, liberty, and the pursuit of happiness and has always been a leader in upholding those ideals in other nations. He claims that protecting democracy in other countries, especially in the nations of Europe, has always benefited the United States by containing the power of its communist enemies. Clinton maintains that Bosnia requires a strong U.S. presence during the tentative peace established by the Dayton Accords.

Good evening. [During the week of November 20, 1995,] the warring factions in Bosnia reached a peace agree-

From Bill Clinton's remarks on Bosnia at a press conference, November 28, 1995.

ment as a result of our efforts in Dayton, Ohio, and the support of our European and Russian partners. Tonight I want to speak with you about implementing the Bosnian peace agreement and why our values and interest as Americans require that we participate.

Life, Liberty, and the Pursuit of Happiness

Let me say at the outset America's role will not be about fighting a war. It will be about helping the people of Bosnia to secure their own peace agreement. Our mission will be limited, focused and under the command of an American general. In fulfilling this mission, we will have the chance to help stop the killing of innocent civilians, especially children, and at the same time to bring stability to central Europe, a region of the world that is vital to our national interests. It is the right thing to do.

From our birth, America has always been more than just a place. America has embodied an idea that has become the ideal for billions of people throughout the world. Our founders said it best: America is about life, liberty and the pursuit of happiness.

In this century, especially, America has done more than simply stand for these ideals, we have acted on them and sacrificed for them. Our people fought two world wars so that freedom could triumph over tyranny. After World War I we pulled back from the world, leaving a vacuum that was filled with the forces of hatred. After World War II we continued, we continued to lead the world. We made the commitments that kept the peace, that helped to spread democracy, that created unparalleled prosperity. And that brought victory in the cold war.

Today, because of our dedication, America's ideals, liberty, democracy and peace, are more and more the aspirations of people everywhere in the world. It is the power of our ideas, even more than our size, our wealth and our military might, that makes America a uniquely trusted nation.

With the cold war over, some people now question the need for our continued active leadership in the world. They believe that much like after World War I America can now step back from the responsibilities of leadership. They argue that to be secure we need only to keep our own borders safe and that the time has come now to leave to others the hard work of leadership beyond our borders.

I strongly disagree. As the cold war gives way to the global village, our leadership is needed more than ever because problems that start beyond our borders can quickly become problems within them. We're all vulnerable to the organized forces of intolerance and destruction, terrorism, ethnic, religious and regional rivalries, the spread of organized crime and weapons of mass destruction and drug trafficking. Just as surely as Fascism and Communism these forces also threaten freedom and democracy, peace and prosperity. And they too demand American leadership.

But nowhere has the argument for our leadership been more clearly justified than in the struggle to stop or prevent war and civil violence. From Iraq to Haiti, from South Africa to Korea, from the Middle East to Northern Ireland, we have stood up for peace and freedom because it's in our interest to do so and because it is the right thing to do. Now that doesn't mean we can solve every problem.

My duty as President is to match the demands for American leadership to our strategic interests and to our ability to make a difference. America cannot and must not be the world's policeman. We cannot stop all war for all time but we can stop some wars. We cannot save all women and all children. But we can save many of them. We can't do everything, but we must do what we can. There are times and places where our leadership can mean the difference between peace and war and where we can defend our fundamental values as a people and serve our most basic strategic interests. My fellow Americans, in this new era there are still times when America and America alone can and should make the difference for peace.

The terrible war in Bosnia is such a case. Nowhere today is the need for American leadership more stark or more immediate than in Bosnia. For nearly four years a terrible war has torn Bosnia apart. Horrors we prayed had been banished from Europe forever have been seared into our minds again: skeletal prisoners caged behind barbed-wire fences, women and girls raped as a tool of war, defenseless men and boys shot down in the mass graves, evoking visions of World War II concentration camps, and endless lines of refugees marching toward a future of despair.

When I took office, some were urging immediate intervention in the conflict. I decided that American ground troops should not fight a war in Bosnia because the United States could not force peace on Bosnia's warring ethnic groups: the Serbs, Croats and Muslims.

Instead, America has worked with our European allies in searching for peace, stopping the war from spreading and easing the suffering of the Bosnian people. We imposed tough economic sanctions on Serbia. We used our air power to conduct the longest humanitarian airlift in history and to enforce a no-fly zone that took the war out of the skies. We helped to make peace between two of the three warring parties: the Muslims and the Croats.

But as the months of war turned into years, it became clear that Europe alone could not end the conflict. This summer, Bosnian Serb shelling once again turned Bosnia's playgrounds and marketplaces into killing fields.

Airstrikes and Diplomacy

In response the United States led the North Atlantic Treaty Organization's (NATO's) heavy and continuous airstrikes, many of them flown by skilled and brave American pilots. Those airstrikes, together with the renewed determination of our European partners and the Bosnian and Croat gains on the battlefield, convinced the Serbs finally to start thinking about making peace.

At the same time, the United States initiated an intensive diplomatic effort that forged a Bosnia-wide cease-fire and got the parties to agree to the basic principles of peace. Three dedicated American diplomats: Bob Frasure, Joe Kruzell and Nelson Drew lost their lives in that effort. Tonight, we remember their sacrifice and that of their families. And we will never forget their exceptional service to our nation.

Finally, just three weeks ago, the Muslims, Croats and Serbs came to Dayton, Ohio, in America's heartland, to negotiate a settlement. There, exhausted by war, they made a commitment to peace. They agreed to put down their guns, to preserve Bosnia as a single state, to investigate and prosecute war criminals, to protect the human rights of all citizens, to try to build a peaceful, democratic future.

And they asked for America's help as they implement this peace agreement. America has a responsibility to answer that request, to help to turn this moment of hope into an enduring reality.

To do that, troops from our country and around the world would go into Bosnia to give them the confidence and support they need to implement their peace plan. I refuse to send American troops to fight a war in Bosnia, but I believe we must help to secure the Bosnian peace.

An End to the Suffering

I want you to know tonight what is at stake, exactly what our troops will be asked to accomplish, and why we must carry out our responsibility to help implement the peace agreement. Implementing the agreement in Bosnia can end the terrible suffering of the people: the warfare, the mass executions, the ethnic cleansing, the campaigns of rape and terror. Let us never forget a quarter of a million men, women and children have been shelled, shot and tortured to death. Two million people—half of the population—were forced from their homes and into a miserable life as refugees. And these faceless numbers had millions of real personal tragedies, for each of the war's victims was a mother or daughter, father or son, a brother or sister.

Now the war is over. American leadership created the chance to build a peace and stop the suffering. Securing peace in Bosnia will also help to build a free and stable Europe. Bosnia lies at the very heart of Europe next door to many of its fragile new democracies and some of our closest allies. Generations of Americans have understood that Europe's freedom and Europe's stability is vital to our own national security. That's why we fought two wars in Europe. That's why we [instituted] the Marshall Plan [which provided American economic aid to Europe after World War II] to restore Europe. That's why we created NATO and waged the cold war. And that's why we must help the nations of Europe to end their worst nightmare since World War II now.

The only force capable of getting this job done is NATO, the powerful military alliance of democracies that has guaranteed our security for a half century now. And as NATO's leader and the primary broker of the peace agreement, the United States must be an essential part of the mission. If we're not there, NATO will not be there. The peace will collapse, the war will reignite, the slaughter of innocents will begin again. A conflict that already has claimed so many victims, could spread like poison throughout the region, eat away at Europe's stability and erode our partnership with our European allies.

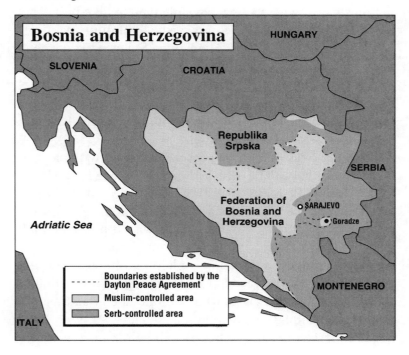

And America's commitment to leadership will be questioned, if we refuse to participate in implementing a peace agreement we brokered right here in the United States, especially since the Presidents of Bosnia, Croatia and Serbia all asked us to participate and all pledge their best efforts to the security of our troops.

When America's partnerships are weak and our leadership is in doubt it undermines our ability to secure our interests and to convince others to work with us. If we do maintain our partnerships and our leadership, we need not act alone. As we saw in the Gulf War and in Haiti, many other nations who share our goals will also share our burdens. But when America does not lead the consequences can be very grave, not only for others but eventually for us as well.

An International Force for Peace

As I speak to you, NATO is completing its planning for IFOR, an international force for peace in Bosnia of about 60,000 troops. Already more than 25 other nations, including our major NATO allies, have pledged to take part. They will contribute about two-thirds of the total implementation force, some 40,000 troops. The United States will contribute the rest, about 20,000 soldiers. Later this week, the final NATO plan will be submitted to me for review and approval. Let me make clear what I expect it to include and what it must include for me to give final approval to the participation of our armed forces.

First, the mission will be precisely defined with clear realistic goals that can be achieved in a definite period of time. Our troops will make sure that each side withdraws its forces behind the front lines and keeps them there. They will maintain the cease-fire to prevent the war from accidentally starting again. These efforts in turn will help to create a secure environment so that the people of Bosnia can return to their homes, vote in free elections and begin to rebuild their lives. Our joint chiefs of staff have concluded that this mission should and will take about one year.

Second, the risks to our troops will be minimized. American troops will take their orders from the American general who commands NATO. They will be heavily armed and thoroughly trained. By making an overwhelming show of force they will lessen the need to use force. But unlike the U.N. forces they will have the authority to respond immediately and the training and equipment to respond with overwhelming force to any threat to their own safety or any violations of the military provisions of the peace agreement.

If the NATO plan meets with my approval I will immediately send it to Congress and request its support. I will also authorize the participation of a small number of American troops in a NATO advance mission that will lay the groundwork for IFOR. Starting some time next week they will establish headquarters and set up the sophisticated communications systems that must be in place before NATO could send in its troops, tanks and trucks to Bosnia.

The implementation force itself would begin deploying in Bosnia in the days following the formal signature of the peace agreement in mid-December. The international community will help to implement arms control provisions of the agreement so that future hostilities are less likely and armaments are limited while the world community, the United States and others, will also make sure that the Bosnian Federation has the means to defend itself once IFOR withdraws. IFOR will not be a part of this effort.

Civilian agencies from around the world will begin a separate program of humanitarian relief and reconstruction, principally paid for by our European allies and other interested countries. This effort is also absolutely essential to making the peace endure. It will bring the people of Bosnia the food, shelter, clothing and medicine so many have been denied for so long. It will help them to rebuild, to rebuild their roads and schools, their power plants and hospitals, their factories and shops. It will reunite children with their parents and families with their homes. It will allow the Bosnians freely to choose their own leaders. It will give all the people of Bosnia a much greater stake in peace than war so that peace takes on a life and a logic of its own.

The Risks

In Bosnia we can and will succeed because our mission is clear and limited and our troops are strong and very well prepared. But, my fellow Americans, no deployment of American troops is risk-free and this one may well involve casualties. There may be accidents in the field or incidents with people who have not given up their hatred. I will take every measure possible to minimize these risks but we must be prepared for that possibility.

As President my most difficult duty is to put the men and women who volunteered to serve our nation in harm's way when our interest and values demand it. I assume full responsibility for any harm that may come to them. But anyone contemplating any action that would endanger our troops should know this: America protects its own. Anyone—anyone—who takes on our troops will suffer the consequences. We will fight fire with fire, and then some.

After so much bloodshed and loss, after so many outrageous acts of inhuman brutality, it will take an extraordinary effort of will for the people of Bosnia to pull themselves from their past and start building a future of peace. But with our leadership and the commitment of our allies the people of Bosnia can have the chance to decide their future in peace. They have a chance to remind the world that just a few short years ago the mosques and churches of Sarajevo were a shining symbol of multi-ethnic tolerance, that Bosnia once found unity in its diversity. Indeed, the cemetery in the center of the city was just a few short years ago, the magnificent stadium which hosted the Olympics, our universal symbol of peace and harmony.

Bosnia can be that kind of place again. We must not turn our backs on Bosnia now.

And so I ask all Americans, and I ask every member of Congress—Democrat and Republican alike—to make the choice for peace. In the choice between peace and war, America must choose peace.

My fellow Americans, I ask you to think just for a moment

about this century that is drawing to a close and the new one that will soon begin. Because previous generations of Americans stood up for freedom and because we continue to do so, the American people are more secure and more prosperous. And all around the world more people than ever before live in freedom. More people than ever before are treated with dignity. More people than ever before can hope to build a better life. That is what America's leadership is all about.

We know that these are the blessings of freedom and America has always been freedom's greatest champion. If we continue to do everything we can to share these blessings with people around the world, if we continue to be leaders for peace, then the next century can be the greatest time our nation has ever known.

A few weeks ago, I was privileged to spend some time with His Holiness Pope John Paul II when he came to America. At the very end of our meeting, the Pope looked at me and said, "I have lived through most of this century. I remember that it began with a war in Sarajevo. Mr. President, you must not let it end with a war in Sarajevo."

In Bosnia this terrible war has challenged our interests and troubled our souls. Thankfully we can do something about it. I say again, our mission will be clear, limited and achievable. The people of Bosnia, our NATO allies and people all around the world are now looking to America for leadership. So let us lead. That is our responsibility as Americans.

Good night and God bless America.

Keeping the Peace

Jeff Stinchcomb

When the Dayton Peace Accords finally established peace in Bosnia in 1995, the United States sent soldiers to the region in order to enforce the agreement and maintain stability. Jeff Stinchcomb, a military reservist, was stationed in Bosnia during the NATO peacekeeping efforts in 2000. In the following editorial, Stinchcomb reports on the various reactions he received as an American soldier in Bosnia. He discovered that many Bosnians—especially Serbs—hated Americans and resented foreign intervention in their affairs. On the other hand, Stinchcomb met some Bosnians who thought that American peacekeepers were enforcing the peace in a professional and effective manner. Stinchcomb also spoke with Bosnian children who had begun to feel more optimistic about the future due to the peace established by American soldiers.

T he soccer field is pristine, lush and green, trimmed like no fairway ever was—a solitary patch of loveliness in a valley desecrated by killers.

Ethnic Slaughter

In 1995, a U.S. satellite passing overhead photographed about 600 people held prisoners on this field, just outside the town of Nova Kasaba in northeastern Bosnia.

The next day, the field was empty.

Additional photos revealed scars made by a tractor in an adjacent meadow. Freshly turned patches of earth—coupled with witness accounts—led analysts to conclude the field contained a mass grave.

Reprinted from "Ground Truth," by Jeff Stinchcomb, *The San Diego Union-Tribune*, May 28, 2000, by permission of the author.

Within a month, the photos would be used to justify U.S. intervention in Bosnia-Herzegovina. After three years of ethnic slaughter, America was stirred to action by an atrocity viewed from space.

[In the summer of 1999], wearing a sergeant's rank on my collar, I stood less than a mile from that field, sweating profusely, sharing an orange soda and a little shade with a hard-line Serb in Nova Kasaba.

"Americans like to play cowboys, putting your noses in everyone's business," he said. "I wish you would have let us play cowboys and Indians with the Muslims for another year."

As he spoke, forensic investigators continued digging near the soccer field, reaping the grisliest of harvests—the dead.

"What are they doing out there," the man went on, "digging up our neighbors?"

It was this moment—more than any other—that defined my reason for coming to Bosnia. More than the hours spent talking with young widows, the parents of murdered sons, abandoned pensioners, veterans who show their wounds on street corners.

Nova Kasaba sits in a narrow river valley between Srebrenica and Tuzla. When Srebrenica fell to the Bosnian Serb Army in July 1995, some of its residents escaped into the forests where they headed northwest for Tuzla. Instead, many found ambushes and mine fields, capture and execution.

The line between Srebrenica and Tuzla is said to be littered with the dead.

Much like Nova Kasaba.

Conflict and Intervention

Bosnia is the most ethnically diverse state in the former Yugoslavia; its pre-war population was 44 percent Muslim, 31 percent Serb, 17 percent Croat and 8 percent gypsy and others.

For nearly 40 years, the glue of Joseph Broz Tito's repressive policies held Bosnia's ethnic mosaic together. When he died in 1980, the glue dissolved.

When Bosnians voted to secede from Yugoslavia in March

1992, the Serb minority—having inherited the lion's share of Yugoslav weapons in Bosnia—triggered a vicious game of atrocity, counter-atrocity while rapidly seizing territory.

Three years later—after ceding as much as 70 percent of the countryside to the Serbs—Bosnian Muslims and Croats set aside their differences long enough to launch a successful counteroffensive.

It was almost too successful.

Western analysts feared that Serbia proper—nervous in the face of Bosnian Serb losses—would become directly involved and spark a regional conflict affecting Europe.

The offensive added pressure for an American-sponsored peace agreement—the Dayton Peace Accords—and an international peacekeeping force to back it up.

As that force nears its fifth year, politicians and pundits are pondering its usefulness as they debate the future of U.S. involvement overseas. Before passing judgment, they would do well to recall the lives we saved in Bosnia—and those we didn't.

I arrived in Bosnia in the spring of last year. A reservist, I was a member of a four-man Psychological Operations (PSYOP) team—a very small part of the Army's Information Operations scheme to support the Stabilization Force, or SFOR.

My team was tasked with gauging and, ideally, influencing Bosnian opinions of SFOR, for the underlying truth of peacekeeping is this: Without their approval, we are occupiers, not peacekeepers.

We were also tasked with disseminating information to support the Dayton Accords. Everything from mine-awareness coloring books for children to property-rights handbills for refugees—and a slew of print and radio products to promote ethnic tolerance.

Given the nature of our mission, we were uniquely positioned to witness what my commander called "ground truth," to see the wreckage and hear the stories of everyday Bosnians.

For me, their stories held a simple moral: The most precious borders don't surround countries, those sovereign stretches of land, but innocent civilians, people.

More than Just Words

"You can get more with a kind word and a gun than you can with a kind word alone." The words are Al Capone's but the United Nations (U.N.) should have heeded them.

Ironically, U.N. High Commissioner for Bosnia Carl Westendorph used the Capone quote, during his final speech [in July 1999]. Ironic because the U.N. came to Bosnia with kind words, high ideals but not enough resolve to back them up. It failed to halt the killings.

Understandably, baby-blue berets [which U.N. peacekeepers wore] are not *en vogue* in Bosnia.

French Gen. Phillipe Morillon wore the U.N.'s baby blue when he came to Srebrenica and announced: "You are now under the protection of the U.N. forces."

So did Dutch peacekeepers. After the U.N. failed to provide the support to keep that promise, they were forced to turn over fuel for buses that hauled Srebrenica's women away from the fallen enclave.

An estimated 7,000 to 8,000 men and teen-age boys "under the protection of the U.N. forces" weren't allowed to board those buses. They were never seen again.

Except in places like Nova Kasaba.

Different Hats, Different Mission

American soldiers don't wear baby-blue, they wear Kevlar.

Militarily, the American-led SFOR has been successful by maintaining close relations with key Bosnian leaders and by keeping rival factions squarely in its cross-hairs.

And it has paid off.

SFOR kept the peace, if not the quiet, last year in what was the most volatile period since the entry of American troops.

Among the year's developments:

• The controversial Brcko decision was made, in effect, removing exclusive control of the strategic town from the Serbs;

• Nikola Poplasen, hard-line president of the Republika

Srpska, was removed by U.N. High Commissioner Westendorph for failure to support the Dayton Accords;

• Gen. Momir Talic, chief of staff of the Bosnian Serb Army, was arrested for war crimes;

• Yugoslav President Slobodan Milosevic was indicted by the Hague;

• More than 40,000 refugees from Kosovo and Serbia's Sanjac region flooded Bosnia; and

• Air-raid sirens twice called SFOR soldiers to the bunkers as Yugoslav jets and missiles violated Bosnian airspace.

Though some Bosnians were resentful of foreign intrusion, others welcomed the aid which was distributed through local Red Cross centers.

During the North Atlantic Treaty Organization's (NATO) bombing campaign, Bosnian Serbs became enraged. They cursed American troops and called us killers. Kindly old ladies stepped out of Norman Rockwell paintings just to give us the finger.

Younger Serbs were more active. One threw a grenade at an American checkpoint. There was at least one report of sniping and, on a personal note, two men tried to run me down with a car.

Not everyone was so vehement.

One Serb told me SFOR's evenhandedness proved to be

the real peacekeeper during the Kosovo crisis [in 1999 when ethnic Albanians in Kosovo tried to win independence from Serbia] and throughout our Bosnia operation.

In the twilight of an August evening, we talked as he held his three-year-old daughter in his arms. He was from Bijeljena but he and his young wife were visiting family in Vlasenica.

Vlasenica is one of seven *opstinas*, or counties, my team patrolled. The county seat is a bastion of nationalism where graffiti on the wall reads: "Death to Americans" and "Bill send body bags for your soldiers."

Given where we stood, his comments surprised me.

"I have seen a lot of armies," he said. "The Americans are good. Very professional. I don't think anyone else could have stopped us from killing each other."

I asked him if I could write down his name to pass on his comments to my commander. "No," he said. "In Bijeljena, I am in the same kind of work you are. It would be bad for me."

He was a Serb soldier.

Miles to Go

If the military side of the mission has been successful, the fight for the civil and economic recovery of the country has yet to be decided.

It is the hardest aspect of the mission—dozens of humanitarian organizations applying dwindling amounts of aid while trying to encourage refugee resettlement—and dealing with graft at every level of Bosnian government.

Some say it has been an outright failure, that we should pull out and save ourselves heartache and money. Our commitments in Bosnia and Kosovo have made us the world's police force and spent dollars better used for our children at home, they say.

These people have stared too long at maps and television screens—but never peered into the eyes of the people on the ground. Into the faces of abandoned old folks, refugees and widows, gap-toothed children whose only crime was to live in the wrong enclave at a savage point in history.

Maybe I've stared too long at the faces; emotional involvement is a point I'm willing to concede.

Today, America enjoys the most prosperous time in its history. If our overseas commitments are significant, they haven't kept us from buying that new Sports Utility Vehicle or rolling the dice with the latest technology stock.

America has spent vigorously in Bosnia, with money, manpower and even blood, but we have halted the wholesale killing of innocents.

How much is that worth?

The Soldiers' Life

"Tis the soldiers' life
To have their balmy slumbers waked with strife."

The words are William Shakespeare's and they are just as true today as when he penned "Othello." If Bosnia has been a hardship, then it has been soldiers—and their families— who have borne the cost.

More than 90 peacekeepers from the 35-nation force have died in Bosnia since 1995.

In my unit, at least three marriages ended during our deployment. One officer lost his business. A wife raised a newborn son alone while her husband cradled an M-16.

But these sacrifices gave Bosnians and their children a thousand small victories—a chance for a normal life and hope.

How often can a soldier claim so much?

In Bosnia, children come running whenever our convoys stop, peppering the Joes with requests for MREs (Meals Ready to Eat) or treats.

"Pepsi, you give me? Hey you! What you name? Lunch bucket, you give me?"

They are the country's lone bright spot.

Last fall, after a hard afternoon rain chased a group of kids away from our Humvees [armed vehicles], a boy lingered to talk with my interpreter, Darko, and me. "My parents used to go every year to the coast in Dalmatia. I have never seen the ocean. The way things are, I don't think I will ever see it."

He could be talking about the political or ethnic reasons;

more likely, he is too poor to even dream of such a trip. The ocean is just a myth.

"Sometimes," he says, "I think it would have been better if I had never been born."

This is like being slapped.

I bend over, look this kid in the eye. He is no more than 10. "Don't ever say that," I tell him. "Things are hard now. You are growing up in the hardest time. But it has to get better. Life is a gift. Never forget that—a gift."

Weeks later, our patrol stops in that town again. As we step from our Humvees, the usual suspects run toward us. Instead of pleas for candy or Pepsi, one yells out something different.

Without preamble, Darko, tilts his head and says: "'Life is a gift.'"

A sweet moment.

But you couldn't see it from space.

Chronology

1314–1353
The Bosnian kingdom emerges.

1325
Under the leadership of Stephen Kotromanic, Bosnia acquires the principality of Hum, later called Herzegovina.

1353–1391
Tvrtko I reigns in Bosnia during the high point of the medieval Bosnian kingdom, which, after 1377, includes much of Serbia.

1389
Turks from the Ottoman Empire push west into the Balkans, defeating a united Balkan force in the Battle of Kosovo.

1398
Turks invade Bosnia.

1463
The Ottomans conquer Bosnia.

1500s–1800s
Turkish rule prevails in Bosnia and the entire Balkan region, except for Slovenia and Croatia, which are under the control of Hungary and Austria.

1878
The Austro-Hungarian Empire conquers Bosnia; the Treaties of San Stefan and Berlin recognize Serbia as an independent kingdom.

1914

Archduke Ferdinand of Austria is assassinated by a Serbian, initiating the First World War.

1918

The Austro-Hungarian and Ottoman empires dissolve at the end of World War I; the first Yugoslav state is formed under the Serbian Karadjordjevic dynasty.

1929

Serbian king Alexander abolishes the Yugoslav constitution and declares a royal dictatorship over Yugoslavia.

1939

The Second World War begins in Europe.

1941

Germany, Italy, Hungary, and Bulgaria invade Yugoslavia; the independent state of Croatia is formed under Axis auspices; extremist Croatian nationalists called the Ustase murder Serbs and Jews, and extremist Serbian nationalists called the Chetniks massacre Muslims and Croats.

1941–1945

Yugoslav partisans, led by Marshal Tito, successfully resist the Ustase.

1945

World War II ends; the Federal People's Republic of Yugoslavia, later renamed the Socialist Federal Republic of Yugoslavia, is established and led by Tito.

1948

Tito is expelled from the communist alliance, Cominform, by Soviet leader Joseph Stalin, and Soviet domination over Yugoslavia ends.

1950s

Tito breaks with Soviet-style communism and establishes a more open form of communism.

1980

Tito dies and is succeeded by a rotating presidency drawn from Yugoslavia's six republics and two provinces.

1987

Slobodan Milosevic wins control of Serbia's League of Communists and begins his rise to power.

1990

The Soviet Union collapses, initiating the demise of communism in Eastern Europe; the power of communists in Yugoslavia diminishes, weakening the glue that had held together the diverse Balkan peoples; multiparty rule begins in Bosnia.

April: Slovenia and Croatia hold the first multiparty elections; Croatia elects nationalist Franjo Tudjman, and an anti-Serb campaign begins in Croatia.

August: An armed conflict breaks out between the Croatian government and Krajina Serbs who, desiring independence from Croatia, proclaim the Krajina region of Croatia the Croatian Serb Republic.

1991

March: War between the Croatian Serbs and Croatia heats up; Tudjman and Milosevic discuss dividing up Bosnia between Croatia and Serbia; each claims to be reclaiming territory that used to belong to it before Tito created Bosnia.

June: Slovenia and Croatia declare independence from Yugoslavia; the Yugoslav army attacks Slovenia but quickly withdraws; war begins between Yugoslavia and Croatia.

September: Macedonia declares independence; the United Nations Security Council (UNSC) imposes an arms embargo on all Yugoslav republics in an effort to head off armed conflicts.

1992

January: Led by Radovan Karadzic, Bosnian Serbs declare the Serb Republic of Bosnia; the European Community (EC) recognizes Slovenian and Croatian independence; United Nations (UN) special envoy Cyrus Vance brokers a cease-fire in Croatia.

February: An EC peace conference on Bosnia proposes partitioning the state into three ethnic cantons in order to avoid secession and war, but Bosnian president Alija Izetbegovic opposes the plan.

March: Bosnia declares independence; war breaks out between Serbs, Croats, and Muslims in Bosnia. United Nations peacekeeping forces are sent to Bosnia at Izetbegovic's request.

April: The EC and the United States recognize Bosnia's independence; Bosnian Serbs begin siege of Sarajevo; Serbia and Montenegro form the Yugoslav federation.

May: The UN admits Slovenia, Croatia, and Bosnia but refuses to recognize the new Yugoslavia, consisting of Serbia and Montenegro; the Sarajevo breadline massacre is blamed on the Serbs, which results in a UN economic embargo against Yugoslavia; the Yugoslav National Army (JNA) sides with the Serb militia in fighting against the Muslims in Bosnia; the first allegations of ethnic cleansing in Bosnia are made by the U.S. State Department.

July: Bosnian Croats, who wanted independence from Muslim-dominated Bosnia, declare the Croatian state of Herceg-Bosna.

August: Serb-run concentration camps are discovered, and systematic rapes of Muslim women are reported.

October: The UNSC establishes a "no-fly" zone over Bosnia.

1993

January: Cyrus Vance and EC mediator David Owen present a plan to carve Bosnia into ten ethnic provinces with a weak central government, but only the Bosnian Croats accept the plan.

March: Under pressure from the United States, the Bosnian government accepts all parts of the Vance-Owen plan, but the Serbs do not; finally, Karadzic agrees to sign the plan.

April: Bosnian Serb "parliament" rejects the Vance-Owen plan; fighting breaks out between Bosnian Croats and Muslims in western Bosnia.

May: The UNSC establishes an international war crimes tribunal in the Hague to investigate crimes in former Yugoslavia.

June: The Krajina Serbs vote for union with the Bosnian Serb Republic; the Vance-Owen plan is shelved.

July: The North Atlantic Treaty Organization (NATO) deploys combat aircraft in Italy to carry out the UN's threatened air strikes against Serbs if fighting does not cease.

August: Owen announces the Geneva plan for partitioning Bosnia into three ethnic states, but the Bosnian parliament rejects the plan.

1994

February: The Bosnian government and Croatian Defense Council commanders agree on a cease-fire accord; four Bosnian Serb aircraft violate the UN ban on military aircraft over Bosnia and are downed by NATO fighters.

March: Izetbegovic and Tudjman sign an agreement to link Bosnia and Croatia in a confederation.

April: NATO planes bomb Bosnian Serb positions.

May: The United States passes the Dole-Lieberman amendment to unilaterally lift the UN arms embargo on Bosnia.

June: Cease-fire talks begin at Geneva, and all parties agree to a month-long cease-fire; the UN reports continued ethnic cleansing of non-Serbs in Banja Luka in Bosnia; armed conflict in Bosnia is reported to be more intense than before the cease-fire.

1995

May: An eleven-judge international tribunal to prosecute war crimes in Bosnia hears the first case against a Bosnian Serb, Dusan Tadic, who was indicted for committing atrocities against Muslims.

August: U.S. president Bill Clinton employs American and allied airpower against the Serbs; the Federal Republic of Yugoslavia (Serbia and Montenegro) is authorized to sign the Dayton peace plan on behalf of the Bosnian Serbs.

September: The allied bombing campaign forces the Bosnian Serbs to agree to a peace talk, and the bombing is suspended; all parties honor a cease-fire agreement; peace talks begin in Dayton, Ohio.

November: All parties in the conflict sign the Dayton Peace Accords, officially bringing the Bosnian war to an end.

1999

In May, Milosevic is indicted by the Hague War Crimes Tribunal for deporting 740,000 Kosovo Albanians and for murdering 340 others between January 1, 1999, and late May 1999; Milosevic remains free because the tribunal lacks the power to bring the Serbian president to trial.

2001

February: The UN war crimes tribunal in the Hague convicts three former Bosnian Serb commanders of rape and torture and establishes sexual enslavement as a crime against humanity.

March: Milosevic is arrested by Serbian Special Forces on corruption charges; his arrest is the first step in bringing him to trial for war crimes committed in Bosnia, Croatia, and Kosovo during the Balkan wars.

For Further Research

Books

Rabia Ali and Lawrence Lifschultz, eds., *Why Bosnia?* Stony Creek, CT: Pamphleteer's Press, 1993.

Phyllis Auty, *Tito*. New York: McGraw-Hill, 1970.

Ellen Blackman, *Harvest in the Snow: My Crusade to Rescue the Lost Children of Bosnia*. Washington, DC: Brassey's, 1997.

Anna Cataldi, *Letters from Sarajevo*. Trans. Avril Bardoni. Rockport, MD: Element Press, 1993.

Stephen Clissold, ed., *A Short History of Yugoslavia*. London: Cambridge University Press, 1966.

Roger Cohen, *Hearts Grown Brutal: Sagas of Sarajevo*. New York: Random House, 1998.

Phillip Corwin, *Dubious Mandate: A Memoir of the UN in Bosnia*. Durham, North Carolina: Duke University Press, 1999.

Zlatko Dizdarević, *Portraits of Sarajevo*. New York: Fromm International, 1994.

———, *A War Journal*. Trans. Anselm Hollo. New York: Fromm International, 1993.

Robert J. Donia and John V.A. Fine Jr., *Bosnia and Hercegovina: A Tradition Betrayed*. New York: Columbia University Press, 1994.

Zlata Filipovic, *Zlata's Diary*. Trans. Christian Pribichevich-Zorich. New York: Viking, 1994.

Misha Glenny, *The Fall of Yugoslavia: The Third Balkan War*. New York: Penguin Books, 1996.

Roy Gutman, *A Witness to Genocide*. New York: Macmillan, 1993.

Peter Handke, *A Journey to the Rivers: Justice for Serbia.* New York: Viking Penguin, 1997.

Richard Holbrooke, *To End a War.* New York: Random House, 1998.

Jan Willem Honig, *Srebrenica: Record of a War Crime.* New York: Penguin Books, 1997.

Rezak Hukanović, *The Tenth Circle of Hell: A Memoir of Life in the Death Camps of Bosnia.* New York: Basic Books, 1996.

Robert Kaplan, *Balkan Ghosts: A Journey Through History.* New York: Vintage Books, 1993.

Radha Kumer, *Divide and Fall? Bosnia in the Annals of Partitian.* London: Verso, 1997.

Florence Hamlish Levinsohn, *Belgrade: Among the Serbs.* Chicago: Ivan R. Dee, 1994.

Anthony Loyd, *My War Gone By, I Miss It So.* New York: Atlantic Monthly Press, 1999.

Sonia Lucarelli, *The International Community and the Yugoslav Crisis: A Chronology of Events.* Florence, Italy: European History Institute, 1995.

Peter Maass, *Love Thy Neighbor: A Story of War.* New York: Vintage Books, 1997.

Branka Magas, *The Destruction of Yugoslavia.* London: Verson, 1993.

Noel Malcolm, *Bosnia: A Short History.* New York: New York University Press, 1994.

David Owen, *Balkan Odyssey.* New York: Harcourt Brace, 1995.

Sabrina Petra Ramet, *Balkan Babel: The Disintegration of Yugoslavia from the Death of Tito to Ethnic War.* Boulder, CO: Westview Press, 1992.

Edward R. Ricciuti, *War in Yugoslavia.* Brookfield, CT: Millbrook Press, 1993.

David Rieff, *Slaughterhouse: Bosnia and the Failure of the West*. New York: Simon & Schuster, 1995.

Mesa Selimovic, *Death and the Dervish*. Trans. Bogdan Rakic and Stephen M. Dickey. Evanston, IL: Northwestern University Press, 1996.

Laura Silber and Allan Little, *Yugoslavia: Death of a Nation*. New York: Penguin Books, 1997.

Fred Singleton, *A Short History of the Yugoslav Peoples*. Cambridge, England: Cambridge University Press, 1989.

Elma Softić, *Sarajevo Days, Sarajevo Nights*. Trans. Nada Conic. Saint Paul, MN: Hungry Minds Press, 1996.

Chuck Sudetic, *Blood and Vengeance: One Family's Story of the War in Bosnia*. New York: W.W. Norton, 1998.

Jasminka Udovicki and James Ridgeway, eds., *Burn This House: The Making and Unmaking of Yugoslavia*. Durham, NC, and London: Duke University Press, 1997.

Ed Vulliamy, *Seasons in Hell: Understanding Bosnia's War*. New York: St. Martin's Press, 1994.

Warren Zimmermann, *Origins of a Catastrophe*. New York: Random House, 1996.

Periodicals

Edward Barnes, "Behind the Serbian Lines," *Time,* May 17, 1993.

Mark Bartolini, "Mortars by Candlelight in Sarajevo," *New York Times,* December 24, 1994.

Karen Brewslav, "When Marriage Is Sleeping with the Enemy," *Newsweek,* October 5, 1992.

Roger Cohen, "Ex-Guard for Serbs Tells of Grisly 'Cleansing Camp,'" *New York Times,* August 1, 1994.

———, "Muslim's Ordeal Shows How Ethnic Lines Harden," *New York Times,* August 30, 1994.

Lyn Cryderman, "In the Camps," *Christianity Today,* February 8, 1993.

Zlatko Dizdarević, "Under the Gun in Sarajevo," *Time,* February 21, 1994.

James L. Graff, "The Butcher of the Balkans," *Time,* June 8, 1992.

————, "The Road of White Death," *Time,* March 15, 1993.

Michael Montgomery, "Flight of Terror," *Time,* April 12, 1993.

Jill Smolowe, "The Human Cost of War," *Time,* November 25, 1991.

————, "Land of Slaughter," *Time,* June 8, 1992.

U.S. News & World Report, "The Serbian Spoiler," May 20, 1996.

Lally Weymouth, "The Strongman of Serbia Speaks," *Newsweek,* December 21, 1998.

Naida Zecevic, "Will I Ever Go Home Again?" *Newsweek,* March 8, 1993.

Index